SOCIAL EVOLUTION

SOCIAL EVOLUTION

BY
PROF. V. GORDON CHILDE

With a Foreword by
SIR MORTIMER WHEELER

LONDON
C. A. WATTS & CO. LTD.

This book is based on a series of lectures delivered at the University of Birmingham in 1947-8 under the Josiah Mason Lectureship founded by the Rationalist Press Association

First published 1951
Second impression 1951
Third impression 1952
Revised & reprinted 1963

Printed in Great Britain by William Collins Sons and Co. Ltd., London and Glasgow, and published by C. A. Watts & Co., Limited, 39 Parker Street, Kingsway, London, W.C.2

FOREWORD

It is a dozen years since my old friend, the late Gordon Childe, passed the proofs of this book, and much has happened in the interim. Nevertheless, his main thesis remains remarkably intact and is likely to endure as a landmark in the study of the evolution of society. From time to time and from mind to mind as new evidence appears there will inevitably be changes of bias or fashion, and some of Childe's political and social philosophy is indeed already a little dated. But it is well that the book should now be republished, and I have been glad, at the publisher's invitation, to re-read it with an eye to anachronism. In the process I have preferred here and there to omit rather than to re-write; but I would make it clear that most of the text stands as it was printed in 1951.

My few modifications are as follows.

On p. 33, in defining the transition from Savagery to Barbarism Childe associated the latter stage, as we all now do if we use the Childe terminology, with the introduction of food-production. But he continues: " Yet a case can be made out for the retention of Morgan's criterion—pottery. . . ." Since 1951 the evidence for a widespread pre-pottery or non-pottery food-producing phase (which may or may not justify the sobriquet " Neolithic ") has accumulated from Cyprus, Jordan, Iraq and Pakistan, and there is no doubt that Childe would to-day have omitted the invention of pot-making as a mark of the advance of Barbarism over Savagery. I have accordingly cut the relevant sentences, together with the opposite affirmation that " pots were made by some food-gatherers,

5

and it is probable that in some regions they were so made before any Neolithic farmers had reached the vicinity." In other words, the relationship of pottery to food-production is nowadays a local problem, not a facet of a general principle.

More difficult is it to readjust Childe's complicated definition of the next stage, Civilization (pp. 34 ff.). To " the progressive enlargement of the unit of cohabitation " and " the accumulation of a social surplus " he adds a third criterion, " the invention of writing." Two discoveries since 1951 have complicated this synthesis. First the excavation of the 10-acre pre-pottery walled settlement at Jericho by Dr. Kathleen Kenyon has now, on Carbon 14 dating, carried the first two criteria back to the 8th millennium—far beyond the known introduction of writing (late 4th millennium). Secondly, a year after the publication of *Social Evolution* Michael Ventris announced his interpretation of a widespread Mycenæan syllabary, at Knossos and on the Greek mainland, thus invalidating Mycenæan Greece as Childe's " choice example of an advanced barbarism " and promoting it (on his definition) to the category of Civilization. Whether Childe would have accepted this transfer, or whether, with his usual open-mindedness, he would have loosened his definition of " Civilization ", is of course beyond conjecture. From my knowledge of him I am inclined to believe that he might have taken the latter course; his original definition was certainly a trifle tight and exclusive.

But the immediate result of these discoveries, if we allow Childe to adhere rigidly (as we obviously must in his own book) to his definition of Civilization, is to disqualify pp. 46-53 of his 1951 edition. Those pages contain an interesting excursus on Mycenæan Greece and Homer as a presentation of ripe barbarism. I have compromised by excising them from the text, to which they can no longer belong, and by consigning them to an appendix (pp. 179-185) for purposes of record.

Less important, on p. 133 I have added a few words to bring the reference to Knossos more nearly into harmony with present thinking. The general sense of the text is not affected.

1962   *Mortimer Wheeler*

CONTENTS

PREFACE

When I was honoured by the invitation to deliver the
Josiah Mason Lectures in Anthropology, I was somewhat
at a loss, being a prehistoric archæologist, but archæologists
today have realized that they are dealing with the concrete
remains of societies, and that these societies, albeit
illiterate, have left concrete embodiments not only of
their material equipment but also of their social institutions, superstitions, and behaviour, fragmentary and
ambiguous though these undoubtedly be. Accordingly, I
thought that the theory of social evolution, deduced by
Herbert Spencer and Lewis H. Morgan from the comparative study of existing societies, might usefully be
examined in the light of the science which presents
societies in a chronological sequence. The results of a
preliminary and provisional examination were presented
in the lectures printed here. If those results seem mainly
negative, and certainly unfavourable to any theory of
unilineal evolution, some positive conclusions did emerge
which were to me unexpected and which may, I hope,
prove interesting and stimulating to the reader.

V. GORDON CHILDE

August, 1950

ABBREVIATIONS

Acta Arch.	*Acta Archæologica*, Copenhagen.
A.J.A.	*American Journal of Archæology*, Bryn Mawr (Archæological Institute of America).
Ant. J.	*Antiquaries Journal*, London (Society of Antiquaries).
J.N.E.S.	*Journal of Near Eastern Studies*, Oriental Institute, Chicago.
K.S.	*Kratkie Soobshcheniya o dokladakh i polevykh issledovaniyakh*, Instituta Istorii Materialnoi Kultury, Moskva-Leningrad.
P.P.S.	*Proceedings of the Prehistoric Society*, Cambridge.
Real.	*Reallexikon der Vorgeschichte*, edited by Max Ebert, Berlin.
S.A.	*Sovietskaya Arkheologiya*, Leningrad-Moscow.

CHAPTER I

Evolutionary Theory in Ethnography

In using the phrase "social evolution," students of the science of man—anthropology in the widest sense—have mistaken "evolution" for a sort of generalized magic force that does the work of the concrete individual factors that shape the course of history. To understand and correct this misapprehension it is useful to begin with the history of the phrase and its implications.

The idea, like its name, has of course been borrowed from Natural History. In that domain the systems of Linnæus and Bouffon in the eighteenth century had already set out phyla, orders, and genera of living organisms in an arrangement that was to some extent hierarchic. In the last year of that century Lamarck enunciated the theory that this hierarchy was the result of a natural process—an evolution. Species and genera had not been miraculously created all at once and immutable, but one species had evolved out of another earlier and lower species by a natural process—and that meant a process intelligible to human reason. The theory was in effect from the first a rationalist protest against theological dogmas of supernatural intervention. But the mechanism—inheritance of acquired characteristics—proposed to account for evolution proved incompatible with observed facts. So "transformism," or "evolutionism," made little progress till Darwin and Wallace propounded a better mechanism and amassed a convincing body of observations in support thereof.

But by 1859 Darwin could not only adduce his own

13

observations to demonstrate variation; he could also appeal to palæontology to prove the historicity of the process. Whereas in the contemporary world all sorts of organisms from amœbæ to mammals exist side by side, in the record of the rocks those phyla, orders, and genera that were ranked higher in the evolutionary hierarchy actually make their first appearance later than those ranked lower down. Now, in stratigraphical geology " later than " means " higher up than " in an undisturbed sequence of sedimentary deposits. So the terms " higher " and " lower " in organic evolution acquired an objective meaning and were emancipated from their anthropocentric subjectivity. *Homo sapiens* became the highest mammal not only by his own prejudice, but as the latest species to emerge.

In the eighteenth century, too, savants were becoming better acquainted with human societies fundamentally different from European, and were recognizing among " savages " an unexpected variety of social structures, economies, and technologies. Some at least recognized grades of " savagery." As early as 1768 Ferguson[1] contrasted " savagery " with " barbarism " and both with " civilization." Indeed, the ethnographers of the eighteenth century sought to introduce order—and that an hierarchic one modelled on the *Systema Naturæ*—into the growing mass of odd customs, rites, and beliefs that were being recorded with ever greater accuracy.[2] By 1850 Herbert Spencer in his *Social Statics* had adumbrated an analogy between Society and Organism, an analogy tediously elaborated in the *Principles of Sociology*. His conception of supraorganic evolutions is based on this analogy. As organisms " grow," so do societies; though, as he rightly insists, the factors determining growth are different. Ex-

---

[1] *Essay on the History of Civil Society* (Edinburgh; 1768).
[2] Cf. Radcliffe-Brown, *Amer. Anthr.*, XLVIII (1946), 233 ff.

isting savage, or barbarous, societies have been arrested
in their growth, and so illustrate early stages in the growth
of abstract Society. Spencer clearly regards this growth
as a process in time. He admits, of course, that "though
taking the entire assemblage of societies, evolution is inevitable, it cannot be held inevitable in each particular society
or indeed probable" (*Principles,* p. 107).

But evolution can be described in general laws which,
on his assumptions, can be deduced from observation of
an actual historical process. So he repeatedly appeals to
contemporary "primitive" societies as illustrating stages
in this temporal process. On p. 103 we read:

When the higher intellectual powers it inherits from
civilized ancestors begin to act, and when its stage of
mental development represents that of such semi-
civilized races as the Malayo-Polynesians. . . .

Or again:

[Slavery] begins unobtrusively: the Patagonians for
instance make slaves of women and children taken in
war. Later, especially when cannibalism ceases, comes
the enslavement of male captives (p. 491).

In practice, of course, Spencer dipped rather uncritically
into a capacious bag of not unimpeachable ethnographic
data. I cannot find that he had systematically arranged
the societies he quotes as instances in any sequence of
stages. So he ought not to claim that his illustrations are
factual data for the induction of the rule they illustrate.
The order of arrangement is based, if on anything more
than a prejudice in favour of bourgeois democracy, on
the alleged analogy with an organism. It would be the
latter that in the long run determines the rank of any
society in Spencer's hierarchy.

Herbert Spencer had, in fact, seen the need for a comparative sociology or anthropology. The comparison of
societies, both those known from history and those then

being discovered by travellers and missionaries—the future anthropologists—should disclose a hierarchy and thus provide data for the induction of general laws descriptive of the evolution of society in the abstract. But just because of his desire not merely to demonstrate the validity of an evolutionary process but also to establish the actual course of social evolution, his work helped to vitiate anthropology itself for many years. As Forde[1] has recently said :

> By introducing *a priori* stages of evolution which captured the imagination and diverted the attention of anthropologists for two generations, Spencer substituted for the comparative study of actual societies which he advocated in principle, the formulation of hypothetical social conditions in imaginary primeval societies which could be considered plausible starting-points for processes of unilineal evolution by which the more complex historic societies have emerged.

Now, the line of inquiry that Spencer adumbrated on a grand scale, but did not pursue, was subsequently explored in restricted fields by Sir Henry Maine in his Studies on *Ancient Law* (1861), by another lawyer, Bachofen, in respect of kinship systems (*Das Muttereecht,* 1861), by McLennan in the institution of marriage (1886), and by Bucher in economics (1893). All these used ethnographic illustrations for theories on the evolution of institutions. But none justified, or indeed formulated, the principles on which the order of the societies adduced might be objectively based.

E. B. Tylor, the actual founder of the distinctively British school in ethnography, followed the same lines. His assumptions were clearly enough enunciated in 1889 :

> Human institutions, like stratified rocks, succeed each other in series substantially uniform over the Globe, independent of what seem the comparatively super-

[1] *J.R.A.I.,* XVIII (1889), pp. 245-69.

ficial differences of race and language, but shaped by similar human nature.[1]

More explicitly than Spencer he formulated certain postulates that were implicit in his aim and guided his methods:

The conditions of culture among the various societies of mankind, in so far as it is capable of being investigated on general principles, is a subject apt for the study of laws of human thought and action. On the one hand the uniformity which so largely pervades civilization may be ascribed, in great measure, to the uniform action of uniform causes; while on the other its various grades may be regarded as stages of development or evolution, each the outcome of previous history and about to do its proper part in shaping the history of the future (*Primitive Culture*, 1871, p. 1).

Like any other science, comparative ethnography, to discover general laws, must isolate related phenomena and make abstraction from the complex variety of their particular manifestations. So "for the present purpose it appears both possible and desirable to eliminate considerations of hereditary varieties or races of man, and to treat mankind as homogeneous in nature, though placed in different grades of civilization" (p. 7). Ignoring the differences due to heredity, to environment, or to historical "accident," we are left with society as such, obeying general laws.

In studying both the recurrence of special habits or ideas in several districts, and their prevalence within each district, there come before us ever reiterated proofs of regular causation producing the phenomena of human life, and of laws of maintenance and diffusion according to which these phenomena settle into

[1] British Association, Presidential Address to Section H (1947).

permanent standard conditions of society at definite stages of culture (*ibid.*, p. 13).

In practice, however, Tylor introduced a further abstraction. What he compares in the sequel are not human societies as functioning wholes, but isolated activities, or aspects, of societies—not cultures, but components of cultures or culture-traits. And that procedure, already foreshadowed in Spencer, leads, as will appear, to the " threads and patches " theory of culture that has vitiated so much of the work of the English Evolutionists, but was taken over by their leading opponents, the Diffusionists.

At the same time Tylor failed, as conspicuously as Spencer, to establish objectively in advance the positions which the several societies whose beliefs or institutions he compares occupy in his hierarchy of grades.

These errors were to some extent avoided by Lewis Henry Morgan[1] in America. The subject of his investigation is not the evolution of individual institutions isolated from their social context, but the evolution of society as a whole. Secondly, he attempts at the start to determine the order in which the societies that are to document his theses are to be arranged. At least, he laid down in advance the framework of a sequence—the so-called " ethnical periods "—and formulated criteria by which the position of any observable society in the sequence could be recognized. Three " ethnical periods " were distinguished —Savagery, Barbarism, and Civilization—and the first two each sub-divided into three " *status* "—" lower," " middle," and " upper." Finally, the criteria Morgan selected are technological, and therefore comparable to the objects of archæological study. In anthropology archæology must play the same role as palæontology does in zoology.

For the rest, Morgan's principles and assumptions are much the same as those of his English contemporaries,

---

[1] *Ancient Society* (1871), p. 8.

though enunciated with even greater confidence. We can make abstractions of racial and environmental divergences and other historical accidents:

The experience of mankind has run in nearly uniform conditions; human necessities in similar conditions have been substantially the same; the same operations of the mental principle have been uniform in virtue of the brain of all races of mankind. We have the same brain perpetuated by reproduction which worked in the skulls of barbarians and savages in bygone ages. . . . Out of a few germs of thought conceived in the early ages have been evolved all the principal institutions of mankind. . . . The evolution of these germs has been guided by a natural law which formed an essential attribute of the brain itself; its results are uniform, coherent and traceable in all their courses.[1]

Though Morgan, through ignorance of the still infant science of archæology, lacked any evidence of the chronological position of his "ethnical periods," he was even more confident than Tylor that they revealed a genuinely historical process enacted in time:

As it is undeniable that portions of the human race have existed in a state of savagery, other portions in a state of barbarism and still other portions in a state of civilization, it seems equally so that these three distinct conditions are connected with one another in a natural as well as necessary sequence of progress. Moreover, that this sequence has been historically true of the entire human family up to the status attained by each branch, is rendered probable by the conditions under which progress occurs and by the known advancement of several branches of the family through two or more stages of these conditions.[2]

[1] *Ancient Society* (1871), p. 61.
[2] *Ancient Society* (1871), pp. 3-4.

And the whole process could be reconstructed by comparative methods :

The domestic institutions of the barbarous, and even of the savage, ancestors of mankind are still exemplified in portions of the human family with such completeness that, with the exception of the strictly primitive period, the several stages of this progress are tolerably well preserved.[1]

It might be thought that the adoption of technological criteria for the definition of stages in evolution and for the assessment of a society's rank in the evolutionary scale got rid of the subjectivism that infected the English school. What Spencer and Tylor really mean when they describe a political system or a religious belief as higher than another is that it approximates more closely to what in the 1870s was regarded as the ideal form of political organization or religion—in fact, an improved liberal democracy or refined Anglican Christianity. Surely this does not apply to technology. Is not the relative value of a machine or a process determinable objectively, and indeed mathematically, by the efficiency with which it fulfils its function? Alas! this objectivity is spurious. For the function of a technical tool or process is to satisfy a human need. But human need is not a fixed quantity. No doubt the efficiency of an automobile to satisfy the need for transport under specific conditions can be determined with mathematical accuracy. But is man's need for transport a fixed quantity in any real sense? Did a reindeer hunter in 30,000 B.C., or an Ancient Egyptian in 3000, or an Ancient Briton in 30, really need or want to travel a couple of hundred miles at 60 m.p.h.?

Human needs have changed in thirty millennia just as much as the " efficiency " of the instruments for their satisfaction. To a Magdalenian society in the last Ice Age

[1] Ibid., p. 7.

a harpoon of antler was just as efficient as a steam trawler is to-day. With the former, tiny groups could get all the fish they needed; the load of a trawler would have been an embarrassing nuisance. Human needs are not rigid and innate in man since his emergence from the pre-human; they have evolved, if that be the chosen word, as much as everything else. Their evolution has to be traced by comparative and historical methods, just like that of other aspects of the process. Any superiority possessed by an automobile over, say, a bullock-cart cannot be inferred from comparing their respective efficiencies on English roads, but only from the historical fact that automobiles do supersede bullock-carts wherever conditions for their employment can be created. Hence the rank of any technical device or process in the evolutionary hierarchy cannot be deduced from any general principle, but must be inferred from archæological data. The sole advantage of technological over political or ethical criteria is that they are more likely to be recognizable in the archæological record.

The intrinsic importance of Morgan in the history of anthropological theory is enormously enhanced by the circumstance that Karl Marx and Friedrich Engels adopted his scheme. That was no accident. Marx had announced the Materialist Conception of History in 1859[1]—the very year that witnessed the publication of the *Origin of Species* and the vindication of Pleistocene man by John Evans, Falconer, and Prestwich. This conception asserts that the whole structure of society is in the long run determined by the " mode of production " that in turn is dependent on the " means of production "—i.e., on the technical forces at the disposal of society for the satisfaction of socially recognized needs. Marx reached this conclusion from the historical data furnished by civilized societies—classical,

---

[1] *A Contribution to the Critique of Political Economy,* Preface.

medieval, and modern. When he wished to test its applicability to simpler but illiterate societies, Marx, failing personal experience in the ethnographic field, would naturally turn to the work of Morgan.

The latter had collected data of just the kind suited for illustrating the Materialist Conception of History. The criteria he used for distinguishing between savagery, barbarism, and civilization, if not precisely "forces of production"—still less "modes of production"—at least approximated more closely thereto than the criteria expounded by any other school at that time. In the end Engels[1] succeeded brilliantly in correlating the transition from one "status" to the next in Morgan's scheme with changes in the productive forces at the disposal of society. In practice, of course, Engels had to modify Morgan's scheme, not to fit ready-made theories, but in the light of his own deeper knowledge of the relevant results of prehistoric archæology in Europe.

Very substantial alterations have since been made necessary not only by the rapid progress of archæology, but also by the accumulation of more abundant and more accurate accounts of existing savage and barbarous societies. Morgan had in fact very little reliable data to go on. He had himself worked among the Iroquois, and was indeed the discoverer of what he terms the "gentile organization" (what is to-day more often called the clan system) and of the classificatory system of kinship terminology. From the missionary Fison he secured much valuable information on the social organization of the Australian aborigines. By questionnaires that he circulated widely and wisely, he accumulated comparable data on tribes living in America, Africa, and the Pacific. For the rest, like Maine, he relied on classical and biblical authorities.

[1] *Der Ursprung der Familie, des Privateigentums und des Staates, im Anschluss an Lewis H. Morgans Forschungen* (1884).

Fresh data accumulated by more recent field studies, conducted more and more by trained investigators with increasingly refined techniques of observation, have played havoc with the contents of Morgan's scheme. Even his account of the economic and political organization of the Iroquois may need some revision. It would therefore be pointless to-day even to summarize Morgan's (and Engels's) account of the several stages of economic, political, or kinship organization. In detail it is untenable. Yet it remains the best attempt of its kind. In the sequel I shall use Morgan's terminology as a provisional basis of classification, though I shall, of course, propose new criteria.

Nevertheless, the last fifty years have not witnessed a development or refinement of evolutionary theory in anthropology, but rather increasingly bitter criticism of the whole position. And some of this criticism is not only destructive but also instructive.

It will be recalled that the word "evolution," in anthropology as well as in zoology, has been a rallying call for an onslaught on *a priori* dogmas sanctioned by supernatural authority. As long as species were accepted as immutable, each could be regarded as created by a special intervention of providence, and Natural History could thus be squared with the account "revealed" in the first chapter of Genesis. That was the dogma that Darwin shattered. The corresponding dogma in anthropology was based on the story of the Fall of Man. The "scientific" equivalent of the Fall is degradation or degeneration. Tylor had to devote many pages to showing that most of the savages he described were not degenerate groups who had fallen from a hypothetical higher stage of culture, but rather groups who were indeed evolving, but whose evolution had been retarded or even arrested. Of course, he admits degeneration in certain cases, but insists that these cases are exceptions rather than the rule.

In the twentieth century the doctrines of Creation and the Fall have been revived under the guise of Diffusionism. I am sure that Elliot Smith, the founder of the English Diffusionist school, had no intention of reviving theological dogmas in his polemic against Tylor and his concept of evolution. Yet that in effect is what Diffusionism has led to. In its strict form Diffusionism starts from the affirmation of Niebuhr[1] that "No single example can be brought forward of an actually savage people having independently become civilized." Lord Raglan[2] adduces reasons that convince him that "savages never invent or discover anything." Savages are represented by Diffusionists as totally without initiative, without the desire or the capacity for inventing a device, a myth, or an institution. All the major inventions were made but once by some chosen people. From the latter they were diffused through the outer darkness of savagery. The various stages of barbarism are due to radiations from the one focus of civilization—radiations which were accepted in varying degrees but always degraded in the process. Since no people can civilize itself, civilization must be a miracle, the result of supernatural intervention.

Of course, Elliot Smith believed he had rationalized this miracle; a unique conjuncture of circumstances had enabled the Ancient Egyptians to break from the circle of savagery, to create civilization, and to initiate its diffusion. But subsequent archæological discoveries have shown that this rationalization is itself a myth. Metallurgy, for instance, is just as old in Hither Asia as on the Nile. If it were diffused, the Egyptians are more likely to have learnt

[1] "Kein einziges Beyspiel von einem wirklich wilden Volk aufzuweisen ist, welches frey zu Kultur übergegangen wäre," *Römische Geschichte*, I, p. 88.

[2] *How Came Civilization?* (1939), p. 170.

it from Asiatics than *vice versa*. They had opportunities for discovering the secret, but the available evidence is that they did not. And so with the remaining constituents of Egyptian civilization and their relations with the Sumerian. With the elimination of the Nilotic Eden, Diffusionists like Lord Raglan have had to postulate some centre which they cannot identify by positive evidence but have to transfer to some archæological *terra incognita*. But as no plausible regions remain completely unexplored and no explored regions fit the bill, the unique cradle of civilization is fast receding into the celestial sphere.

While Evolutionism must remain a protest against any such revival of mythology, the " conflict " between Evolution and Diffusion is entirely fictitious. Diffusion is a fact. The transfer of materials from one territory to another is archæologically demonstrated from the Old Stone Age onwards. But if material objects can thus be diffused, so can ideas—inventions, myths, artistic designs, institutions. Evolutionists have never denied this. For "evolution " does not purport to describe the mechanism of cultural change. It is not an account of why cultures change —that is the subject-matter of history—but of how they change. When Morgan turned to consider how changes came about in concrete cases, he himself did full justice to the role of evolution.[1]

The Functionalists, representing a reaction against the falsely contrasted methods of evolution and diffusion alike, have levelled constructive criticisms against both. We have already remarked in Tylor a tendency to regard culture as a mechanical assemblage of " traits " that can profitably be isolated and compared with other traits similarly picked out of another culture. The English Diffusionists went so far that they spoke as if they regarded the rank of a cul-

[1] Cf. Leslie A. White, " Diffusion vs. Evolution: An Anti-Evolutionist Fallacy," *Amer. Anthr.*, XLVII (1945), pp. 341 ff.

ture as measured by the number of traits recognizable in it; in any case the " loss " of culture traits was accepted as a sign of degeneration or degradation. That is the "threads-and-patches" theory of culture, against which the Functionalists rightly inveigh.[1] A culture is an organic whole, not a mechanical aggregate of traits. You cannot legitimately isolate one component in Australia or Hither Asia, label it " totemism " or " wheeled vehicle," and then compare this abstraction with something formally similar in Canada or Egypt, and so deduce its origin and evaluate the status of the culture to which it belongs. You must first see how it works, discover its place in the life of the society concerned. Only then will it help to a comparative evaluation of the two societies. For instance, in the narrow valley of Egypt, where habitable land was seldom even two miles away from the admirable highway of the Nile, wheeled vehicles would not be anything like so useful as on the steppes of North Syria, which lack natural waterways. The fact that wheeled carts were used in the latter area fifteen hundred years earlier than in Egypt does not mean that Egypt was more " backward " than Syria.

Equally justly the Functionalists point out that all schools of comparative ethnographers have arranged the societies they compare in a hierarchical series on quite arbitrary principles. The order is not given in observation but is based an prejudices. Of the Evolutionists Piddington can justly say:[2]

> The basic fallacy lies in the unjustified transition from an observable logical-geographical scheme to a hypothetical chronological one. This means selecting from different contemporary communities a series of customs or social forms which might conceivably have

[1] Radcliffe-Brown, " The Concept of Function in Social Anthropology," *Amer. Anthr.*, XXXVII (1935), p. 401.
[2] Reviewing Landtman, *The Origin of Inequality of Social Classes,* in *Man*, No. 54 (1940).

followed one another within a single community or in human history as a whole. No human community is any "lower," "earlier," or "more ancient" than any other. All represent highly specialized human adaptations, the product of millennia of traditionalized cultural life.

Archæology offers an escape from the dilemma stated by Piddington. The evolutionary series of organisms, postulated by Lamarck, was converted into a historical series by palæontology; the record of the stratified rocks revealed the chronological order in which the several phyla, orders, and genera actually did appear. Can archæology render a comparable service to the evolutionists in anthropology? The prehistorians' cultures represent, albeit imperfectly, societies. These cultures are no longer regarded as lifeless assemblages of accidentally connected types. A culture is the durable material expression of an adaptation to an environment, human as well as physiographical, that enabled a society to survive and develop. From this point of view the buildings, tools, weapons, ornaments, and other surviving constituents are interrelated as elements in a functioning whole.

Now the archæological record discloses sequences of such cultures, stratigraphically established, in several areas. In other words, it reveals the chronological order in which societies have appeared. How far does this "observable scheme" really provide the basis for a "logical" one? Let us compare homotaxial cultures—that is, cultures occupying the same relative positions in the several observed sequences—to ascertain whether the agreements between them can be generalized as stages in cultural evolution, the evolution of Society in the abstract.

CHAPTER II

The Classification of Societies in Archæology

Archæology can establish sequences of cultures in various natural regions. And these cultures represent societies or phases in the development of societies. Potentially, therefore, archæological sequences reveal the chronological order in which kinds of society did historically emerge. But to realize this potentiality the several cultures or societies, each of which is concretely distinct and individual, must be classified on some more general and abstract principles. Now, prehistorians do in fact apply such a general classification to their cultures in the Old World, assigning them respectively to the Stone, Bronze, or Iron Age (or Stage). How far is the current archæological classification serviceable for the present purpose—that is, to trace the evolution of social organisms?

The classification into the Three Ages[1] was originally devised for archæological objects, relics and monuments, in order to show which of them belonged together. The terms Stone, Bronze, and Iron Ages go back to a Dane, Thomsen, who about 1812 used them for the arrangement and classification of exhibits in the newly-founded Museum of Northern Antiquities at Copenhagen. Thomsen had decided to group together objects made and used in the same period of time. No written records were available to show when the illiterate inhabitants of Denmark made and used the objects to be catalogued and exhibited. But Thomsen knew that bronze had been used for cutting-tools and weapons before iron, and stone before bronze.

[1] Cf. G. A. Daniel, The Three Ages (Cambridge: 1942).

All objects current before bronze came into use were therefore classified in the first division and labelled " Stone Age." All objects, of whatever material, found in graves or otherwise associated with bronze swords, spears, or axes, were labelled " Bronze Age," and so on.

This classification was adopted in other European countries, for it was found that in Great Britain, France, Switzerland, Italy, and Germany also, stone was used for weapons and tools before bronze, and bronze before iron. By the crucial year 1859, the division of prehistoric European antiquities among the three ages was generally accepted. But by that year it appeared that the first division was of unwieldy size. It contained rude implements found in old river gravels of Pleistocene age, as well as the much finer and more varied tools and weapons from the Swiss lake-dwellings and the megalithic tombs of Denmark. So the Stone Age had to be subdivided. Lubbock proposed the principle of division that in the sequel won universal acceptance. He termed " Palæolithic," or Old Stone Age, those implements found in association with remains of extinct and always wild animals, and sharpened by chipping but never by grinding. On the other hand, those found accompanied exclusively by the bones of recent animals—including domestic species—and sometimes sharpened by grinding or polishing, he labelled " Neolithic," or New Stone Age.

Note that Thomsen's division had been essentially technological—the material used for the principal cutting-utensils. Lubbock abandoned this simplicity and admitted chronological and economic criteria in addition to the technological. He thought all three coincided; but in fact they do not. The Palæolithic was equated in the first instance with the Pleistocene, a period of geological time. Secondly, it was an economic stage, a time when people lived exclusively by hunting, fishing, and collecting, before plants were cultivated, or animals bred, for food. Thirdly, the Neolithic was distinguished from the Palæolithic by the employment of polishing to supplement chipping in giving an edge to stone axes and adzes. Stratigraphical observations had shown by 1899 that these criteria do not coincide, and the discrepancy led—but not till 1920!—to a further division of the Stone Age. By 1900 cultures were known belonging to the geological Recent, but still without domestic animals or cultivated plants and polished stone implements. To accommodate them a "Mesolithic," or Middle Stone Age, was ultimately created.[1]

This innovation can only be regarded as deplorable. For it sanctioned and stereotyped a confusion foreign to the minds of the founders of the Three Age system. Thomsen had to arrange the prehistoric material from a small and homogeneous area. In Denmark Stone, Bronze, and Iron described real Ages—periods of time which followed one another in that order. Because the same sequence was observed in other parts of Europe and eventually in Egypt and Hither Asia, it did not follow that the several "Ages" were everywhere contemporary. Thomsen probably never envisaged this possibility. His immediate successors, like Worsaae,[2] explicitly denied it; the Bronze Age began in Egypt and the Eastern Mediterranean much earlier than in the North.

But with Lubbock's division of the Stone Age, one half of it had been identified with a geological period, the Pleistocene. Now, geological periods are applicable to the whole terrestrial globe. Proterozoic, Cambrian, Eocene, Pleistocene denote periods in the history of the

[1] The term was already used by Torell at the Congrès international d'Anthropologie et d'Archéologie préhistoriques in Stockholm in 1874, but became established only after 1921.

[2] "Des Ages de la pierre et du bronze dans l'Ancien et le Nouveau Monde," *Materiaux pour l'Historie primitive de l'Homme* (Paris; 1882), pp. 163-70.

Earth as a whole—i.e., periods of absolute time. That is
patently not the case with the later archæological "Ages."
The Maoris of New Zealand were still in a Stone Age
when Captain Cook arrived in the eighteenth century A.D.
The Stone Age in Egypt had ended before 3000 B.C.!
There is in fact no such thing as *the* Stone Age. There
was *a* Stone Age in England, in Palestine, and in New
Zealand, and it still exists in parts of New Guinea, but
chronologically, as periods of absolute time, they are all
different. On the other hand, the several Ages are everywhere homotaxial, to use a term proposed by T. H.
Huxley.[1] Each, that is, always occupies the same relative
position in the sequence wherever the full sequence is
available. (In New Zealand, for example, the sequence
is incomplete, since the Bronze Age is totally missing.)

The confusion between relative and absolute chronology
has proved itself a tenacious source of error in prehistory.
It might have been avoided had the word "Stages" been
substitute for "Ages." But, provided their relativity be
borne in mind, the Ages may be used as a convenient, but
essentially provisional, framework for the subsequent ex-
position. A further reservation, however, must be made.

Thomsen had classified together things that were found
together or, more technically, associated. They were associated because they were in use at the same time. But for
artifacts to be regularly associated it is necessary that they
should be in use not only at the same time but also by the
same people. Now, even in so small an area as Denmark
local archæologists had found by 1898 that two quite different assemblages of weapons and ornaments were being
used in the New Stone Age, and indeed in the same part
of that Age. Pots, axes, arrow-heads and ornaments of
one class were regularly found in megalithic tombs con-

---

[1] In his Presidential Address to the Geological Society in 1862,
reprinted in *Collected Essays,* vol. viii.

taining the skeletons of many persons buried in the same family vault. Vases, axes, and ornaments of a quite different kind came from individual graves, each containing a single corpse and normally covered by a barrow. These arbitrary differences in burial practice, in the shapes and decoration of vessels, in arms and toilet articles, were not due to differences in time or in the materials available. They must have been determined by the divergent social traditions of distinct peoples. Recurrent assemblages of the kind just described are what archæologists term "cultures."

Prehistorians now recognize that their first business is to classify their relics and monuments into cultures and only thereafter to classify the cultures. But cultures represent societies, as their distinctive characters are due entirely to social traditions. In classifying cultures into one of Thomsen's Ages they are classifying societies. So Thomsen's scheme allows us to arrange societies in a chronological sequence, or rather sequences.

But for comparing cultures in the different sequences the Age classification is useless. To repeat in other words what was said on p. 31, the label "Bronze Age" has no absolute chronological meaning; it is no help if we want to compare an Egyptian culture with a contemporary culture in England. But does this term give any clue as to the technical, economic, or even political development of the society thus labelled? I have spent twenty years trying to give some such values to the traditional "Ages" and to make these archæological stages coincide with what sociologists and comparative ethnographers recognized as main stages in cultural evolution. So in 1925,[1] adopting an idea advanced by Elliot Smith ten years earlier, from the three current criteria (polishing of stone, or modern fauna,

[1] *Dawn of European Civilization,* first edition.

or domestic animals and cultivated plants) I selected "food-production" as distinguishing the Neolithic from the earlier Palæolithic and Mesolithic. Obviously the cultivation of edible plants, the breeding of animals for food, or the combination of both pursuits in mixed farming, did represent a revolutionary advance in human economy. It permitted a substantial expansion of population. It made possible and even necessary the production of a social surplus. It provided at least the germs of capital. And since animals and plants may be regarded as biochemical mechanisms, in cultivating and breeding them men were for the first time controlling and utilizing sources of energy other than those provided by their own bodies.

If stages of economic and social evolution are to be defined on technological bases, food-production should surely mark the beginning of a major stage. I propose therefore to use it to define the transition from Savagery to Barbarism, and so far to allow Barbarism and Neolithic to coincide. But do they in fact completely coincide? In other words, can the next archæological age be equated with the highest stage in ethnographical evolution—namely, Civilization?

As the technological criterion of the latest and highest of his "ethnical periods" Morgan took writing. I find it a very useful criterion. It may indeed seem odd that writing should be included in technology. But, after all, writing is a tool—an intellectual tool, if you will. It was the necessary instrument of exact science, the applications of which have revolutionized technology. Its use led to calendrical astronomy, predictive arithmetic, and geometry—tools demonstrably used by the first civilized societies in the Old and New Worlds, by the Egyptians, the Sumerians, and the Mayas. At the same time a consideration of these earliest literate societies reveals that writing is a

S.E.

C

convenient and easily recognizable index of a quite revolutionary change in the scale of the community's size, economy, and social organization.[1]

The invention of writing seems to coincide with a critical point in the progressive enlargement of the unit of cohabitation and in the accumulation of a social surplus. This critical point should be definable numerically, but at the time of writing the data for estimating with any sort of precision the population of any Egyptian, Sumerian, or Maya city have not yet been disclosed by excavation. Still, it can be seen that, by comparing the area of a Sumerian city with that of any Neolithic village, or the numbers of graves in an early historic cemetery on the Nile with those belonging too preliterate communities (pp. 114, 139), the aggregations of population designated cities represent a new order of magnitude. The character of the population was also novel. It included in all cases, even in Central America, a relatively substantial number of full-time specialists—that is, of persons who did not themselves grow, catch, or collect their own food but were supported by the surplus above domestic needs produced by farmers, fishers, and huntsmen, who themselves became to that extent specialists. Moreover, the former comprised not only artisans and craftsmen but also rulers, officials, priests, and clerks. Again, the citizens were supplied not only with the local products collected from a considerable area around the city but also with materials brought from long distances by regular and organized trade.

In 1930 I attempted to rehabilitate the archæologists' Bronze Age as a major stage in economic as well as merely technological development.[2] In the first place it marks, perhaps, the beginning of specialization of labour —what Engels more accurately designates " the separa-

---

[1] Childe, *Man Makes Himself.*
[2] *The Bronze Age* (Cambridge; 1930).

tion of handicraft from agriculture." Some sort of specialization may exist or have existed in Neolithic socities. Prehistoric flint-miners in England and Belgium were doubtless specialists. In ethnography we find specialist makers of pottery or betel-pouches among societies in the Pacific that are essentially Neolithic. But in neither case are we necessarily dealing with full-time specialists. The potters on the Amphlett Islands and the pouch-makers on the Trobriands[1] also fish and cultivate their gardens. They ply their handicraft in the spare time left over from the essential occupation of getting their own food. The European flint-miners most probably combined mining with cultivating and herding. Such are only part-time specialists. But on ethnographic evidence smiths are generally full-time specialists; they neither grow nor catch their own food, but get it in return for the products of their craft. As far as archæological evidence can go, this applies to prehistoric bronze-smiths. They are the first full-time specialists attested in human history.

Secondly, the regular use of copper or bronze was possible only in so far as regular trade was organized. Trade in the sense of transmission of commodities from one group to another is indeed quite well attested in the Stone Age, even in the Old Stone Age. But the objects of Stone Age trade were always luxuries—if not merely shells or similar "ornaments," at least things that men could easily have done without. A Stone Age community was, at least potentially, self-sufficing. In so far as a society is dependent on copper or bronze for weapons or tools, it has sacrificed this self-sufficiency and is obliged to rely on trade for necessities.

Thirdly, metal did really extend man's control over the external environment, particularly by providing tools that could not be made of wood, bone, or stone. The saw is

[1] Malinowski, *Coral Gardens and Their Magic* (1937).

such a tool, and the saw is apparently essential for making wheels. Both the wheeled cart and the potter's wheel make their debut among Bronze Age societies. Thus the use of metal was responsible for the greatest recorded advance in transportation (at least until the invention of the aeroplane) and for the initiation of the mass production of commodities with the aid of rotating machines; for that is what the potter's wheel meant.

Nevertheless, on closer examination Bronze Age societies in the Old World are found to differ enormously among themselves in their political and social organization, in their economic structure, and even in their level of technological achievement. Many Bronze Age villages in temperate Europe and even in Asia Minor are no larger, nor apparently more articulated, than Neolithic hamlets in the same region. On the other hand, Bronze Age Egyptians, Sumerians, Minoans, and Chinese were fully literate and dwelt often in large cities. So this one archæological Stage covers two major ethnographic or sociological Stages— Barbarism and Civilization, as these terms have just been defined.

It cannot even be contended that the use of metal—for instance, in imposing industrial specialization and trade or by making advanced transport available—was an essential precondition for Civilization. For in the New World the Mayas,[1] in virtue of their refined calendar and their hieroglyphic writing, must be deemed to have reached that status. Yet on archæological criteria they must be labelled Neolithic, since they made no use of metal for tools or weapons. Indeed, they lacked wheeled vehicles or any means of land transport superior to porterage, while their rural economy was based on slash-and-burn cultivation (the so-called *milta* system), an extravagant method that had been superseded by plough agriculture with a

[1] Morley, *The Ancient Maya,* Stamford (1946).

regular rotation long before the rise of any Civilization in temperate Europe.

Accordingly the archæological division between the three Ages provides no serviceable basis for a subdivision of Barbarism into stages. Consequently our Soviet colleagues during the 1930s abandoned not only Thomsen's old division but also any attempt to find a better technological basis for classifying archæological cultures. Instead of Palæolithic, Neolithic, Bronze Age, and Iron Age, they spoke of "pre-clan society" (*dorodovoe obshchestvo*), clan or gentile society (*rodovoe obshchestvo*), and class society (*klassevoe obshchestvo*).

The last term corresponds approximately to Morgan's Civilization, since all civilized societies have been divided into two classes—a small minority that annexes, concentrates, and accumulates the social surplus, and the masses of peasants, artisans, and labourers who at best retain just as much of the product of their labour as is required for domestic consumption. Pre-clan society should correspond to Morgan's lower status of Barbarism—a really hypothetical stage in which social "organization" was limited to the natural family conceived as a promiscuous horde. Efimenko[1] seems to have believed that it was actually represented in what archæologists term the Lower Palæolithic, but unfortunately the available data, even in the favourable case of Pekin man, are too exiguous to allow of legitimate inferences as to how men then arranged their sexual life. The rest of the Palæolithic and later prehistoric periods have then somehow to be distributed within Clan Society. As Morgan and Engels believed that the earliest clans were invariably matrilineal, the earlier pre-class cultures (Upper Palæolithic and some Mesolithic at least) were assigned to the stage or "period" of "the matriarchal clan" (*materinskoe rod*). The transition to

[1] *Pervobytnoe Obshchestvo* (Leningrad-Moskva; 1939).

patrilineal organization (which should take place at a point
in the Neolithic when stock-breeding began to rival cultivation or collecting as a basis for the economy) marks the
beginning of the steady decline to Class Society. So all
later archæological stages or ages can be comprised in the
"period of the disintegration of the clan."

Of course, ethnographers now reject the supposed universal priority of matrilineal over patrilineal kinship, and
furthermore deny that the former coincides with such a
preponderance of female influence in public or domestic
affairs as could be labelled matriarchy. But even if the
sequence were what was generally believed when Engels
wrote, it is not easily applicable to archæological data.
Indications as to kinship systems or the social position of
either sex are singularly rare in the archæological record
and often ambiguous at that. Indeed, Russian prehistorians
were by no means agreed as to where the transition should
be put and which societies still enjoyed the complete primitive communism of matriarchy and among which the
clan was already in disruption. Krichevskiĭ[1] in 1933 was
positive that patriarchal organization was established in
Central Europe in Neolithic III, when pastoralism did
become dominant in a farming economy that had already
developed through two phases. Okladnikov,[2] on the contrary, finds it in Siberia already among tribes that still
lived entirely by hunting, fishing, and collecting. Finally
Tretiakov[3] seems to argue that on the Upper Volga patrilineal succession replaced matrilineal at the same time as
stockbreeding and agriculture began to supplement food-
gathering.

[1] " Indogermanskiĭ Vopros arkheologicheske razreshennyĭ," *Izvestia GAIMK*, 100 (1933).
[2] "Arkheol. Dannye o drevneĭsheĭ istorii Pribaĭkaliya," *Vestnik Drevneĭ Istorii* (1938).
[3] " K Istorii doklassogo obshchestva verkhnego Povolzhiya," *Izvestia GAIMK*, 106 (1934).

In fact the Russian scheme of classification assumes in advance precisely what archæological facts have to prove. Archæology offers in various regions sequences of cultures that follow one another. By comparing these cultures it has been able to establish certain generalizations about the technological aspects of culture. It has proved everywhere that stone was used for tools and weapons before any metal, and that copper or bronze was so used, if at all, everywhere before iron. Archæology has again demonstrated in the New World as well as in the Old that the earliest societies always lived exclusively by hunting, fishing, or collecting, while farming invariably begins later. So, too, illiterate farmers always precede literate citizens. Thus in the terms of the definitions accepted on p. 33, Savagery is older than Barbarism, Barbarism is older than Civilization. The very aim of the present inquiry is to see whether any similar generalization can be inferred from the observed successions in respect of other aspects of culture such as kinship systems.

CHAPTER III

Culture in Archæology and Anthropology

The word "culture" has an inconvenient variety of significations. To certain circles culture, spelt with a capital C or even a K, seems restricted to Art (with a capital A), functionless architecture, literature that does not sell, opera —but not of course Gilbert and Sullivan and hardly even Puccini—and so on.

Archæologists use the word in an equally restricted, but totally different, sense. They define a culture as an assemblage of associated traits that recur repeatedly. These traits are mostly material objects, and the archæologist fixes his attention first on those that differ arbitrarily. *Qua* archæologist I should not be concerned so much with the fact of ritual burial, or the use of axes by prehistoric peoples, or the diet of contemporaries, but rather with peculiarities in burial ritual, the form and material of axes, or the shapes of knives and forks. Arbitrary differences between American and English knives and forks would help me to distinguish, even without the aid of literary or spoken evidence, two societies. For these differences are not dependent on our diet, which remains much the same, or on the need for conveying food to the mouth—common to most self-styled civilized peoples—but solely on divergent tradition as to what constitutes good table manners. Variations in burial practices, or the form of axes, or the decoration of pots must likewise be conditioned by the same sort of historical and social divergences rather than by function, physiographical environment, or material.

These somewhat insignificant traits that engross the archæologist's attention so much are thus convenient symbols for distinguishing cultures. Once a few well-associated assemblages have been observed to establish that a given type of pottery, say, is characteristic of a culture or society, then, whenever we find it in another grave or house-foundation, we know that the persons buried or living there belonged to the same society. And each new grave or settlement, often scattered over quite a wide territory, is liable to afford new scraps of evidence as to the activities of the society concerned. For not all the traits of an archæological assemblage are likely to be found together or revealed by a single excavation. The archæological picture of a culture is built up out of many fragments, observed at different places on various occasions, but always associated with one or more of the symbol traits found to be distinctive of that assemblage. This total picture is much richer and more comprehensive than the type fossils that often occupy too much space in technical archæological articles. But it is still constituted mainly of traits that reflect social habits and are conditioned by social traditions.

The anthropologist's conception of culture does not differ in kind from that of the archæologist, but it is much more comprehensive. It comprises all aspects of human behaviour that are not innate reflexes or instincts. It is everything that men derive from nurture, from human society, rather than from nature or the sub-human environment. It includes language and logic, religion and philosophy, morality and law, as well as the manufacture and use of tools, clothes, houses, and even the selection of food to eat. All this men must learn from their fellows in society. The human infant has to learn from parents and seniors how to talk, how to dispose of his excrement, what to eat and how to prepare it, and so on. All these rules belong to the collective tradition, accumulated and preserved by the society into which a human being is born.

All had to be discovered or invented, but society has preserved the original discoveries and inventions, so that its members do not have to find out for themselves by trial and error what to eat and how to procure it, but are taught by other members of the society, older than themselves, who have similarly learnt from their elders. Even the so-called *a priori* truths of arithmetic and geometry had to be discovered by experiment, but they have been recognized so long and have sunk so deeply into the social tradition that they seem to be imposed on the individual's mind as self-evident truths.[1] As societies have lived in different historical environments and have passed through different vicissitudes, their traditions have diverged, and so ethnography reveals a multiplicity of cultures, just as does archæology.

The social traditions that determine culture are expressed in habits of thought and action, in institutions and customs. All these are essentially immaterial, and exist only so long as the society that inculcates, sanctions, and preserves them is alive and active. Thanks to writing, the language, and with it the logic, of civilized societies has been preserved after they have become extinct, and many of their institutions, beliefs, and laws have also survived in fossilized form. The languages of preliterate barbarian societies have perished with them, but not all their cultures. For all culture finds expression in action—action in the material world. It is indeed through action alone that culture is maintained and transmitted; a belief that exists only in somebody's head forms no part of culture and has no existence for history or anthropology. Some of the

[1] Cf. Leslie A. White, "The Locus of Mathematical Reality," *Philosophy of Science*, XIV (1947).

actions dictated by, and expressive of, culture effect durable changes in the material world. All such fall within the purview of archæology. It is indeed just these human actions that have provided the material out of which archæological cultures are constructed.

Doubtless it is the applied science of extinct illiterate societies that has left the most conspicuous impressions on the archæological record. Prehistoric tools, houses, fields, roads, survive to illustrate the practical knowledge possessed by their makers or builders. They represent applications of socially approved discoveries and inventions. At the same time they are indicators of socially approved needs. Not all carnivorous societies have felt a need for knives and forks. In temperate Europe the need for routes trafficable at all seasons first became socially effective under the Roman Empire and was largely forgotten again in the Dark Ages.

But even more immaterial aspects of culture may find durable material expression. The " constitutions "—if that be the right word—of preliterate societies have been irreparably lost. Yet funerary and domestic monuments and their contents may permit legitimate inferences as to the existence or non-existence of chiefs. If religious beliefs have perished, their expressions in the shape of temples, shrines, idols, amulets, may survive. Nay, they may furnish ground for inference as to the extent to which such beliefs were institutionalized under the guidance of professional priests.

In a word, the archæological record is by no means restricted to tools of production and weapons of war. Under suitable conditions we can learn a great deal about the mode of production as well as the means of production. The role of secondary and primary industry and of trade can be estimated from observed facts. The extent of the division of labour and the distribution of the product can be inferred with some confidence. Plausible guesses can be made as to the existence of slaves, the status of women, and the inheritance of property. Even the ideological superstructure can be made the subject of cautious hypotheses.

The nature of the archæological data on which legitimate inferences and sane speculations can be based will be examined more closely in Chapter v. But here and now a warning is needed as to the availability of such data.

Only exhaustive, systematic, and intensive exploration, collection, and excavation, combined with an equally thorough, detailed, and scientific comparison and analysis of the resultant observations, can provide material for such a real resuscitation of extinct cultures. For instance, numerous petrological and chemical analyses are needed to determine correctly the extent and direction of prehistoric trade. Intensive surveys from the air as well as on the ground can alone reveal prehistoric fields or roads. Only the total excavation of complete settlements can provide reliable data for estimating the density of population or deciding whether the community was divided into chiefs and commoners. But very little of the requisite work has yet been undertaken and its distribution is very uneven.

Vast tracts in the Old World are totally unexplored archæologically. In many of the remaining regions a number of cultures have been defined and their sequences established. But these are defined almost exclusively by pottery styles or a limited range of stone or metal types. Of their economy and polity we know nothing. In only a few regions, and even there only for limited epochs, have the conditions for reconstructing cultures as functioning wholes been met at all. In fact, the sort of data requisite for the present inquiry is available, as far as the post-

Pleistocene phase is concerned, only in the temperate zone of Europe—excluding France and the Balkans—in Greece, Egypt, Palestine, Syria, and Mesopotamia.

This unevenness of exploration is a serious handicap if our object be to establish general stages in the evolution of cultures. For a culture is an adaptation to an environment. It owes its specific peculiarities to the geographical setting in which its authors operated—to physiographical relief, rainfall, temperature, soil, vegetation, and natural resources in the form of minerals, plants, animals, waterways, and so on. Herbert Spencer[1] long ago pointed out that the first of the factors controlling the growth of societies was the inorganic and subhuman world. So too Stalin,[2] to quote the leading exponent of Marxism to-day, includes among "the forces of production" determining the structure of a society "the natural resources of its habitat." Hence to discover general laws descriptive of the evolution of all societies we abstract in the first instance the peculiarities due to differences of habitat.

That can best be done by isolating the common features in societies occupying the most varied natural regions. Our complete series from the Old World does not offer anything like the desirable diversity. It is derived only from the temperate woodland zone, the eastern end of the Mediterranean, the belt of steppe in Hither Asia, and subtropical river valleys.

Furthermore, in order to discover inductively general stages in evolution by comparing the observed development of a number of societies we ought to be sure that our instances are really independent societies. Ideally, indeed, we abstract altogether what Spencer called the supra-

[1] *Principles of Sociology* (1874).
[2] "Dialectical and Historical Materialism," Chapter IV of *The History of the Communist Party of the Soviet Union* (B).

organic environment as a factor in the development of society. The goal should apparently be to see how a society develops if left to itself. Whether that is a legitimate aim will be considered later, but whether it is practicable must be asked at once. Even in the Old Stone Age the transport of materials by human agency far from the places where they occur in nature (e.g., cowrie-shells from the Indian Ocean to France) indicates the likelihood of exchange of ideas also over unexpectedly wide areas. Since the Neolithic revolution the diffusion of substances, manufactures, inventions, cult symbols, and decorative motives over the various societies inhabiting the different parts of Europe and Hither Asia is abundantly documented archæologically.

Indeed, some prehistorians seem to regard the external relations of societies—migrations, conquests, wars—as more worthy of study than the actual functioning of the societies themselves. Our colleagues in the U.S.S.R. rightly deprecate this effort to turn prehistory into a poor imitation of old-fashioned political and military history. They have gone so far as to reject migrations almost entirely as factors promoting change in preliterate cultures, but even they have to admit the importance in this connection of diffusion[1]—the transmission of devices and ideas from one people to another by trade or some other form of peaceful intercourse.

After all, they can argue that these historical occasions for, or mechanisms of, cultural and social change do not really distort the course of evolutionary development. For no society can adopt from another a device unless it fits into the culture already developed by that society. For instance, a negro tribe in tropical Africa cannot adopt transport in automobiles unless it has the technical skill

[1] E.g., Krichevskiĭ in Iz Istorii Dunaĭskogo ponizovia," *K.S.*, VIII (1940).

and equipment to construct roads, a political system to maintain and police them, and an economic system to secure and distribute petrol. Moreover, a need for transport, faster and more economical of labour power than porterage, must be socially recognized. Just the same sort of conditions would hold good for the adoption of wheeled carts by a preliterate society inhabiting the forests of temperate Europe. In each case the wheeled vehicle would symbolize a certain stage in the economic and social development of a society, whether the society invented the device for itself or borrowed it from a neighbouring society.

The same sort of argument will apply to institutions. Chiefs cannot rule over a community unless that community can produce a social surplus above the needs of domestic consumption, sufficient to support the chieftain in idleness—i.e., as a full-time ruler. He is not likely to be tolerated unless his rule can confer tangible benefits that the previous system of government, or lack of government, failed to provide. For instance, a chief may be able to ensure defence against troublesome enemies, or may provide protection for visiting merchants and artisans whose services are socially valued, but who could not appeal to the protection provided by the kinship system and sanctioned only by the blood feud. It would therefore be immaterial whether a king arose in response to popular demand, as reputedly happened in Israel, or imposed himself on the people by conquest. The archæological record is seldom explicit as to the mechanism of cultural change, but this obscurity may be quite irrelevant to the order in which cultural changes occur.

A further obscurity may be more troublesome. The boundaries of the several fields of culture do not necessarily coincide. The archæologist has to rely mainly on material culture—instruments of production, transport devices, house plans, fashions of dress, artistic styles—in defining societies. Judged by these criteria, Europe, North America, and Australia might easily seem to enjoy a single culture and therefore to represent a single society. But of course this relatively uniform cultural province is divided into several linguistic provinces, though language is a very important part of culture. It is split into a still larger number of economically and politically independent States, and many sociologists would identify State and society. At the same time each of these States is subdivided into smaller societies that may even cut across political boundaries—into churches and clubs, economic classes and professions, and so on. The dress, housing, diet, and even the language of such groups within a single State often diverge very substantially. An archæologist might take the material culture of each such group as representative of a distinct society. Might not the excavation of a mining village, a seaside resort, and a market town in Wales lead an archæologist of the late third millennium A.D. to assert that Wales had been occupied by three distinct cultures and as many societies? Unless the atomic bombs to be rained on Britain prove inconceivably more destructive than that dropped on Hiroshima, such a mistake is unlikely. Enough buttons, broken teapots, knives and forks, and so on will probably survive to enable the hypothetical Esquimaux excavator to recognize the overriding uniformity of British culture. In any case, no one has been misled by the disparity between the architecture and furniture contained in a workmen's settlement and in the more familiar palaces of Pharaoh and his nobles to attribute the former to a group of barbarian invaders established temporarily on Egyptian soil.

The discrepancy between material culture and language or political allegiance cannot thus be overcome. In North

America ethnography reveals various peoples—for instance, the Plains Indians—virtually indistinguishable in dress and equipment yet speaking unrelated languages.[1] In Mesopotamia archæology during the third millennium B.C. reveals culture, completely homogeneous not only in tools, weapons, dress, housing, and artistic taste but also in religious architecture, burial rites, and even script; but politically the country was, till 2350 B.C., divided into a number of quite autonomous city States often engaged in internecine war. And, incidentally, two different languages—Sumerian and Semitic—were written in the same script as soon as the latter became fully decipherable. Moreover, in each of these autonomous States the contrast in equipment used by the urban population and that used by the rural peasantry was very sharp and was probably associated with differences in social organization and even in dialect. It has been argued[2] that what we have here is not a single society but an urban society, organized territorially, superimposed on a " folk society " still resting on a kinship basis. The same might apply to contemporary societies in Latin America and Mediterranean Europe, if not to our own.

So for the archæologist the unit or society must remain the group enjoying the same culture—i.e., giving concrete expression to common traditions. Such a group may comprise a number of settlements or local communities. Perhaps we might call its members a people, but we should have no right to assume that this people as a whole spoke a single language or acted as a political unit, still less that all its members were related physiologically or belonged to one zoological race. Even so a subjective element enters

[1] Forde, *Habitat, Economy and Society* (1934), p. 47.

[2] E.g., Sol. Tex, " Revolutions and the Process of Civilization," in *Human Origins*: *An Introductory Course in General Anthropology*, Selected Readings, ii (University of Chicago; 1946).

into this definition. Culture and society are abstractions. No two products of handicraft are strictly identical. Every family of craftsmen, and every member of such a family, have their own tricks of style. No two villages yield precisely the same complex of relics and traits. The subjective element comes in in deciding which idiosyncrasies should be ignored in defining a culture. Frankly, it is hard to say which should be disregarded as purely individual and which should be taken as social traits, the differentiæ of new cultures. German and Austrian archæologists have been busily distinguishing new ceramic styles and making them the symbols, and often the eponyms,[1] of new cultures. Plainly there must be limits to this subdivision. In England down to 1928, prehistorians recognized in their "Early Bronze Age" a single culture, archæologically symbolized by one type of pot, termed a "Beaker," and identified with a single invading people, the "Beaker-folk." In 1948 as least four distinct kinds of Beaker have been distinguished and each attributed to different bands of invaders!

Qua prehistorian it is the archæologist's business to go on distinguishing new cultures and to try to fill in his picture of each. The comparative sociologist, on the other hand, may well have to reduce the multiplicity by ignoring certain differences. Of course there are dangers lest by such abstraction really significant divergences may be overlooked. It is in any case better that it should be a deliberate selection from adequate data than that it should be imposed by ignorance and the record's imperfections.

Such then are the limitations to the identification of archæological cultures with societies. If, none the less, we are to treat the observed sequences of cultures as illustra-

---

[1] *Eponym*: the person (historical or mythical) who gives his name to a city, tribe, or people.

tive of the development of societies, the former must be more than mere assemblages of technological processes or even economies within which the processes can work. They must be invested if not with speech—they are mostly forever dumb—at least with institutions. How far can such preliterate cultures be clothed with life?

CHAPTER IV

Some Examples

Before proceeding further I think I should give some examples—favourable examples, I confess—to show how far archæology can reanimate the remains of a preliterate society. For savagery the record certainly affords very adequate data on the economy and also on the artistic expression of superstitions in the Palæolithic Age, but the interpretation of the latter is naturally quite hypothetical, and direct hints as to social structures are almost totally absent. In the less interesting Mesolithic phase that follows the position is not quite so bad. So I shall take a community in the Crimea,[1] certainly older than any farmers in South Russia and, though not necessarily older than the earliest manifestations of the barbarian economy in Hither Asia or Egypt, still just as certainly untouched thereby.

As elsewhere in temperate Europe, Mesolithic culture in the Crimea was less spectacular and perhaps really poorer than the antecedent Palæolithic cultures of the Pleistocene. For with the passing of glacial conditions steppes and tundras had been replaced by forest, and consequently the gregarious herbivores, on the pursuit of which the prosperity of Palæolithic communities had been based, had become extinct or migrated northwards. Human groups found themselves mutually isolated by forests and swamps and obliged to pursue more solitary animals like red deer, roe deer, and boar. Mesolithic Crimeans lived in caves, certainly in small and isolated groups, the numbers of

[1] General accounts—Childe, *Man* (1942), No. 59 (English); Hančar, *Urgeschichte Kaukasiens* (Vienna; 1938), German.

which cannot be accurately estimated. Like their Palæolithic precursors, they lived by hunting and fishing, but
in addition they relied on collecting to a much greater
extent than earlier communities in Europe. Great heaps of
snail-shells are conspicuous in the Crimean cave-dwellings,
as in all contemporary or homotaxial deposits throughout
Europe. Barbed spears, often called harpoons,[1] were demonstrably used for fishing; in the chase the most conspicuous surviving weapon was the bow—or, to be accurate, the
minute flint blades with which the arrows were armed.
But in contrast to Palæolithic societies, and like all other
Mesolithic groups, the huntsmen were assisted in the chase
by dogs. At least, bones of a canid showing features
appropriate to early stages of domestication have been
found in several caves. Of course, in pursuit of forest
game such an animal ally would be particularly handy and
would really earn a reward in the form of offal after a
successful hunt.

Burials afford the sole positive, if admittedly exiguous
and ambiguous, evidence on the structure of Mesolithic
societies. In the Crimea the dead were, sometimes at least,
interred in the caves where they had camped in life. In a
grave in Murzhak koba[2] two bodies had been interred
simultaneously side by side in an extended position. One
skeleton belonged to a man forty to fifty years old, the
other to a woman of twenty to twenty-five, or half her
companion's age. Finger-joints were missing from the
woman's hand and had probably been ritually amputated
—for this form of mutilation is practised by savages in
South America and is attested already in Palæolithic times
by impressions in French caves. The significance of the
simultaneous burial of men and women will be discussed
later. We shall see that, if it does not necessarily imply
either monogamy or *sati* (the compulsion of the wife to

[1] *S.A.,* v, pp. 170-5.   [2] Ibid., v, pp. 160-9.

follow her lord to the future life), it should at least indicate a subordination of the female to the male. The establishment of this at so early a stage is quite important in view of theories of so-called matriarchy in early society.

The Neolithic village of Skara Brae in Orkney[1] consisted of half-a-dozen one-roomed dwellings, each suited to a single natural family, and is the best preserved of half-a-dozen settlements of the same culture recognized on Mainland and the smaller island of Rousay. Its inhabitants lived by breeding cattle and sheep, supplemented by the products of collecting. There is no evidence that they cultivated any cereals, and no fishing-tackle survives, though Skara Brae lies right on the sea-shore. Tools—and ornaments—were made entirely of local materials. Though flint nodules are plentiful on Rousay and were used there, hardly any flint was used at Skara Brae, where an inferior chert was used instead. Indeed, as there were then no trees in Orkney, even furniture—beds and dressers—was made of local stone, which fortunately splits easily into slabs like planks. There is thus no evidence for trade of any kind. Nor have any weapons been discovered suggesting warfare or even hunting.

Each dwelling is furnished with a central hearth, a two-storeyed dresser against the rear wall, and two beds on either side of the hearth. The beds are always capacious, and that on the right is invariably the larger, varying in size from 6 feet 6 inches by 3 feet 6 inches to 5 feet by 2 feet 9 inches. From its dimensions and from recent practices in the Hebrides it may be inferred that the right-hand bed was occupied by the male members of the household, that on the left by the females. In the wall above each bed were cupboards that could serve as keeping-places for the personal possessions of the bed's occupants.

[1] Childe, *Skara Brae* (1934); *Scotland before the Scots* (1946).

Cells in the walls and tanks let into the floor may have held household stores. But all the six dwellings were buried in a midden-heap and connected by roofed passages, the exits to which could be closed by barred doors exactly similar to those giving access to the several dwellings themselves. All six were thus under one roof, and the whole could be styled a house divided into six apartments just as well as a complex of six houses. Outside the complex were a small paved " square " and an isolated " dwelling," differing from the rest in furniture and actually used as a workshop for making and baking pots and for chert-knapping. It may have housed a family of handicraftsmen, but is more likely to have been used as a communal workshop to which members of the several small households repaired to mould and bake their pots, or to chip chert implements; bone tools were sometimes made and certainly used within the individual dwellings. There would thus be no division of labour within the group save that dictated by sex and age. But at least the construction of the sewers that drained the whole complex and the passages that joined up the separate units must have been communal work, performed by collective labour.

As the dwellings are all identical in plan and furniture, and differ only in size, none can be regarded as the residence of a chief. But the largest may have belonged to the senior member or ancestor of the group. The whole society would thus constitute a single enlarged family or clan, led perhaps by a patriarch but co-operating for the same reasons and under the same sanctions as members of a natural family used habitually to do. These Neolithic societies would thus disclose " primitive communism " still operating in an undistorted form.

At this point the author included the Mycenæan culture as an example of an advanced barbarian society which fell

short of his definition of civilization through lack of his
" diagnostic criterion, writing ". More recently a widespread Mycenæan script—Linear B—has been recognized
and partially interpreted. The editor of this edition has
therefore relegated the example to an appendix, as the
author himself would certainly have omitted or drastically
reshaped it.—*M.W.*]

CHAPTER V

The Sociological Interpretation of Archæological Data

In favourable circumstances archæology can, we have just seen, provide considerable evidence for forming a fairly adequate, though always incomplete, picture, not only of the technology but also of the whole economy of a pre-literate society. Social institutions are far more elusive. Yet it is precisely these that are of chief concern to sociology, and the theories of social evolution considered in the first chapter were primarily concerned with the evolution of structure. Social institutions have been classified by Hobhouse, Ginsberg, and Wheeler[1] under the headings of government, justice, the family, rank, property, and war —to which institutional religion (as opposed to "beliefs") should surely be added. The field of each is confessedly not easy to define. All admittedly interact, and among many barbarous and savage tribes to-day their several fields largely overlap; the organs of government and the direction of institutionalized religion, for instance, often coincide. When applied to illiterate or even early civilized societies, the divisions and the terms used descriptively within each lack the sharpness and precision that they possess in European and North American States to-day.

Examples already given show that in certain circumstances, and always with reserve, archæology can provide some indications as to the form of government and of the family, the recognition of rank, the distribution of the social product, and the practice of war. It is never likely

[1] *The Material Culture and Social Institutions of Simpler Peoples* (1926).

to be able to tell us anything about the administration of justice, the penalties used to enforce it, nor the content of any laws, the way in which descent rather than inheritance of property is determined, the effective limitations on the powers of chiefs, or even of the extent of their authority. The content of religious belief and the nature of the prestige conferred by rank are irretrievably lost. Worst of all, negative evidence is worthless; rich graves or palaces may be evidence for the existence of chiefs, but the absence of the evidence cannot be taken as proof that they did not exist. And much of the available evidence is often ambiguous.

As to "government," without inscribed documents we can form no idea at all of the extent of the political units, save very tentatively in two most exceptional cases. For community of culture, at least in the archæological sense, need not mean political unity. In the third millennium lower Mesopotamia displayed a remarkable uniformity in archæological culture, including even the forms of public worship, and actually enjoyed a common language and recognized a number of common deities. But it was divided up among a dozen or more quite independent States that fought each other often and ferociously. Contemporary Egypt, enjoying an equal cultural unity, was also a single State, and in this instance an archæologist can deduce political unification from the single cemetery of royal tombs, without the aid of written records. It would therefore be rash to equate the archæologist's culture with the ethnographer's tribe, if tribe implies a single government, the exclusion of wars (other than blood feuds), and even recognized rights of intermarriage.

The size of the local group can mean only the number of households found living together in the same place. The extent of its territory can hardly ever be inferred directly. When settlements have been continuously occupied and form tells,[1] half the distance between one tell and the next might give an indication of the respective territories. But in Europe, owing to shifting cultivation and the length of archæological periods, it cannot be assumed that two adjacent hamlets are contemporary. One might be the site where the inhabitants of the next had dwelt ten or twelve years earlier.

Within the recognizable unit the only form of government likely to be detectable—or indeed to be expected—is chieftainship. Its existence may be inferred if one house in a settlement is conspicuously larger, more elaborate, and more sumptuously furnished than all the rest; or if, in a cemetery, a few graves are much more richly furnished than the remainder, especially if the structure of the tomb is exceptional or the obsequies have been accompanied by human sacrifice or other distinctive ceremonies. In Champagne[2] collective burial in family ossuaries (depositories for the bones of the dead) cut in the chalk was the normal rite in the Neolithic Age. Some tombs are very elaborate, being divided into chamber and antechamber and sculptured with an effigy of a female personage; these are richly furnished but contain only six to eight skeletons. Others are much simpler and are furnished with poorer gravegoods, but contain forty or fifty skeletons. The former may fairly be regarded as the tombs of chiefly families, the latter as those of commoners. The Mycenæan cemeteries already described would be a fair analogy and justify the inference.

But the decision is not always so simple. Even in the neighbouring Paris basin, collective tombs, this time walled and roofed with great stone slabs that may be sculptured,

---

[1] *Tells*: mounds composed of the debris of successive villages built and rebuilt on the same site.
[2] Childe, *Dawn*, pp. 302-5.

were used by people of the same culture as those buried in the rock-cut sepulchres of the Marne. But all these tombs, as far as the available reports go, seem to have been equally crowded with bones and equally richly, or rather poorly, furnished with gear. It looks as if all members of the social group, let us say clan, had the right to burial therein.

Now, these built tombs of the Paris basin are just one variety of the large class of tombs termed "Megalithic" and including the long barrows of Great Britain.[1] All are artificial ossuaries erected with extravagant labour but with the simplest tools—without crane, windlass, or wheeled vehicles. The stones composing the burial-chamber are often of gigantic size, weighing up to twenty tons, or the covering mound is enormous, extending in many English long barrows for 300 feet and rising fifteen or more feet in height. All were collective burial-places containing several corpses, and in most cases they were certainly used over several generations. In at least one case in England the individual skeletons all exhibited such a "family likeness" as to suggest to qualified anthropologists blood relationship. Yet the number of skeletons bears no relation to the size of the chamber or the covering barrow. The maximum number recorded in the British Isles is fifty, while it often sinks to five; In Denmark, however, more than one hundred skeletons have been found in some Megalithic tombs. Normally each tomb stands alone and corresponds to a single natural area of habitation such as might in the Scottish Highlands and islands have been occupied by a single crofting community. But tombs of one distinctive type, the so-called Boyne culture, do form regular cemeteries in Ireland—sixty-nine tombs at Carrowmore, Sligo, and fourteen on the Bricklieve Mountains in

[1] Childe, *Dawn*, pp. 208-18.

the same county—and on a smaller scale in Caithness and Nairn.[1]

The question at once arises whether all members of the local group, or only chiefs and their families, were entitled to burial in these elaborate sepulchres. There is probably no single answer applicable to all such tombs. In the Boyne group sixty chieftains at Carrowmore seem too many to be credible, so that these tombs should correspond to the commoners' tombs in Mycenæan Greece. On the other hand, in the same culture the exceptionally large, well-built, and finely sculptured tombs of New Grange, Knowth, and Dowth, look like veritable royal sepulchres and must surely be compared to the finer Mycenæan tholoi. Conversely, the crowded tombs of northern Europe or the Paris basin seem like genuine communal burial-places where all members of the social group might find a final resting-place. The difficulty of applying this explanation to British long-barrows is that it is hard to see how a small group—say a family comprising at most three generations—could transport and erect the gigantic stones or heap the fantastic covering mound. The objection to classing them as chieftains' sepulchres is that no contemporary commoners' burials have been discovered. Of course ethnographic examples can be quoted from Africa and elsewhere where ceremonial burial is reserved to chiefs, other corpses being left in the bush to be devoured by wild beasts and birds. But it is equally easy to cite cases where tribesmen, though dispersed over a considerable area, will co-operate in the erection of ceremonial buildings as well as for the performance of rites.

In any case the archæological evidence for chieftainship, whether derived from habitations or burials, gives no clue as to the nature of the authority enjoyed by the " chief,"

[1] Childe, *P.C.B.I.* (1946).

nor as to its source. All we can infer is the existence of persons enjoying exceptional prestige and generally exceptional wealth. Among contemporary savage and barbarian tribes such prestige may be acquired in many ways—by mere seniority, by birth, by supposed magic power, by prowess in war, and so on—and the degree of political power or authority thus conferred varies very widely.

Where, for instance, the members of a single family keep together as one household or economic unit for three or even four generations, the patriarch or matriarch at the head of the household enjoys such prestige. When, as in Bronze Age Britain, we find a single conspicuous burial at the centre of a ring of more normal interments,[1] the central body is likely to have been that of the patriarch or common ancestor of the group, whose junior members were subsequently interred around his grave. In general the most that an archæologist can mean by "chiefs" is persons who monopolize an appreciable fraction at least of the social surplus. But even if these were chiefs exercising political functions, they were not necessarily specialists living entirely on the reward of leadership. Even a Maori chief, though he owed much of his wealth to the gifts traditionally given to him by his followers, and to the labour of the captives taken in war, or awarded to him as leader, owed some to his own labour. So a chief should be not only "hospitable, brave, apt at settling disputes and learned in tribal boundaries," but also "industrious in collecting food, expert in carving, tattooing, and weaving, and clever in building houses, *pas,* and canoes."[2]

If it is difficult to recognize chiefs with certainty in the archæological record, to recognize an aristocracy is much harder. We can find in Africa and Asia plenty of stratified societies generally resulting from conquest in which an

[1] Childe, *Scotland before the Scots,* p. 43.
[2] Goldenweiser, *Anthropology* (1937), p. 384.

aristocracy, usually mainly pastoral, rules a partly tributary and normally agricultural class. Now, from a relatively short period of the Danish Bronze Age[1] we have no fewer than two thousand four hundred barrows covering graves very richly furnished with handsome bronze weapons and ornaments—and of course all bronze had to be imported. These are generally[2] attributed to a warlike aristocracy owning the land and the sea-going boats. But no traces of a lower class have been demonstrated. As Broholm[3] says, domestic sites of this period are unknown, and we have to rely entirely on burials. Naturally the surviving burials from so remote a period represent only a very small fraction of the actual number.

The aristocratic conception has therefore been quite rightly challenged. If the period covered by the burials in question does not exceed two centuries—and that is one authoritative estimate—the challenge would seem justified. But other authorities would spread the burials over five or six centuries, and then it would seem more reasonable to attribute them to a ruling minority. An exactly similar problem is presented by the undoubtedly earlier, but homotaxial and systadial,[4] Wessex culture[5] illustrated by some two hundred rich interments furnished with bronze weapons and ornaments of imported gold, amber, and even Egyptian or Mycenæan fayence. In neither case is certainty possible.

In at least one case the division of society into classes is quite clearly reflected in the archæological record. In Egypt during the historical period, both under the Old and Middle Kingdoms, there is a sharp contrast between the

---

[1] Broholm, *Danmarks Bronsealder* (1946).
[2] E.g., by Brøndsted, *Danmarks Oldtid*, II (1939), p. 10.
[3] Broholm, *Danmarks Bronsealder* (1946), Vol. II.
[4] *Systadial*: representing the same stage in an evolutionary sequence.
[5] Piggott, "The Early Bronze Age in Wessex," *P.P.S.*, IV (1938).

tombs of pharaohs and nobles on the one hand, and those of commoners on the other. They differ in form and ritual, as well as in funerary furniture; and even if we had no texts at all we could recognize that we were dealing with two distinct classes. This may be due to the exceptional importance attached to burial by Egyptian society, and may therefore be unique. In Babylonia and Assyria only the contrast between royal and ordinary tombs can be recognized, but this, if not due to the inadequacy of the archæological record, might be held to mean that the richer landowners and higher priests did not constitute a distinct class with a recognized social status.

Of course, in all cemeteries differences in the furniture of individual graves can be observed and doubtless indicate differences in wealth, but they are graded differences, so that while the adornments of the poorest and the richest grave may be far apart, there is no point between them where one can say the lower class ends and the upper class begins. Such graded differences in wealth are observable even in the Egyptian cemeteries of commoners.

If chiefs and aristocracies are difficult to recognize archæologically, slaves are even more elusive. It is not till late Iron Age cultures, already in contact with civilized States, that gang chains provide unambiguous archæological evidence. But even earlier burials sometimes provide rather dubious hints. The victims sacrificed at the obsequies of chiefs need not be slaves; it is notorious that barbarians sometimes desire the privilege of following their leader to the other world. But let us distinguish in terms: we occasionally have cases where two corpses of the same sex have been interred together—one with substantial funerary offerings, the other with none. In this case the latter may quite probably have been a slave. Even so, it may be remarked that in two well-attested Scottish cases[1] both skeletons be-

[1] Childe, *Scotland before the Scots*, p. 43.

longed to men of the same physical type—the intrusive Beaker race. It seems hardly likely that the not very numerous invaders would have made slaves of one another.

Another division—that due to specialization of labour—may cut right across that caused by rank. In the ethnographic record specialists, in the sense of experts who are specially skilled in carving weapons, net-making, potting, or some other craft—or for that matter in magic or tribal lore—have been reported at almost all economic levels save the lowest. But generally such are only part-time specialists;[1] they are primarily hunters, or fishers, or farmers, and exercise their special skill not in place of getting their own food directly, but in addition thereto, and in return merely for a supplement to the produce of their own labour. Such part-time specialists could not be recognized in the archæological record and are perhaps not very important for a stadial classification. Full-time specialists are those who do not themselves produce food, but are fed from the social surplus in return for the exercise or products of their special skill. They are not appreciably easier to recognise archæologically, but have generally to be inferred from ethnographic and historical analogies. On the latter grounds, metal-workers and potters who use the wheel are admitted to be probably specialists, and a few other crafts may be distinctly recognized in urban agglomerations. In other preliterate societies we shall probably be justified in refusing to assume full-time specialists.

On the other hand, archæological evidence is available for intercommunal specialization. Even in Neolithic cultures we know communities of flint-miners and axe-factories whose products were widely exported. The miners and axe-makers were doubtless specialists, but can we legitimately compare their settlements to mining villages or

[1] Chapple and Coon, *Principles of Anthropology*, p. 254.

factory towns to-day? Such intercommunal specialization is a familiar phenomenon among contemporary barbarians, for instance in Melanesia. But we do not find that the basket-makers of Luya in the Trobriands[1] or the Amphlet potters gave up tilling their fields or fishing in order to devote their lives to making vases or boxes for betel-nut. They plied their craft in addition to pursuing these primary avocations, and merely increased their wealth in food or commodities by bartering the products. Despite their miserable equipment, the flint-miners of Grimes' Graves in Norfolk or of Spiennes in Belgium should have had ample time to tend their herds and even cultivate small cornplots as well as sinking shafts and fashioning axes from the nodules extracted.

The natural family of parents and children is a biological necessity that archæologists may assume without question. But the family as an institution, a unit of co-operation, and a vehicle for the transmission of property and status, is a quite different matter, and may vary surprisingly. Descent may be reckoned through mother or through father, or even through both parents. There is naturally no superficial clue to enable us to distinguish matrilinear from patrilinear kinship archæologically. But a school of sociologists has held that matrilinear succession confers on the women a higher status than they enjoy in the more familiar patriarchal societies and would indeed almost reverse the roles of the two sexes. This conception of "matriarchy" seems in reality to be exaggerated.[2] In most matrilinear societies it is the maternal uncle rather than the mother who exercises the prerogatives of the father in respect of

[1] Malinowski, *Coral Gardens*, p. 41.
[2] Cf. Lowie, *Primitive Society* (1921); Bonhaar, *Woman in Primitive Mother-right Societies* (The Hague; 1931). But cf. Thomson, *The Prehistoric Aegean* (1949), pp. 150-60.

the children and family property. It is only among a very few tribes like the Khasi in Assam and the Iroquois and some other American Indians, that the wife owns the house and property and can in general take the lead. Yet even among the Iroquois the chief was always a male, though "the matron had everything to do in connection with the selection of a successor as well as his appointment as chief" (Goldenweiser).

In any case, the archæologist could not hope to recognize the supposed prerogatives of matriarchy. Yet small effigies of a female personage have been taken as indications of such. These figurines were carved in soft stone or mammoth ivory by Upper Palæolithic savages; modelled in clay or carved in stone or bone, they were very common among early Neolithic societies. Among some societies they were still manufactured in modern historical contexts. Not only the numerous figurines of Ishtar from Babylonia and Assyria and those of Venus from Greece and Rome, but also contemporary statuettes of the Virgin can be traced back directly to the prehistoric figurines of the Neolithic age at least. Whether the latter indicate the worship of a goddess conceived in female form, as their historical descendants undoubtedly do, may reasonably be questioned. They are at least symptomatic of some fertility ritual based on a recognition of the generative powers of women. As neither male personages nor phalli were thus represented in Palæolithic and early Neolithic cultures, it may be assumed that, as among some contemporary tribes, the part of the father in reproduction had not yet been appreciated. Phallic symbols first appear in Bronze Age or contemporary and adjacent late Neolithic cultures. But in themselves are female figurines any better evidence for matriarchy than are the Venus figures and Virgins of undeniably patriarchal societies?

Rather more positive if still ambiguous evidence as to the status of the sexes is afforded by burials. Graves containing a male and female buried simultaneously, though always unusual, are widely distributed in space and time.[1] There are examples as far back as Neolithic times from the Crimea and Brittany[2] and among later hunter-fisher tribes in Siberia, in the Amratian phase of predynastic Egypt (none in the earlier Badarian),[3] and in the al' Ubaid phase of Mesopotamia.[4] In temperate Europe they are common in the Neolithic age cultures, especially in the later ones, and thereafter down to the Viking age, while a royal tomb at Dendra affords a good example for Mycenæan Greece. Such double burials are generally interpreted as cases of *sati,* whereby the wife is compelled to follow her lord to the future life, and this interpretation seems justified by textual evidence in some late instances— among the Iron Age Kelts and the Vikings, for example. Moreover, in one grave among later hunter-fishers in Siberia it was established that the woman, who was accompanied by an infant, had been shot to death with arrows.[5]

A patriarchal, if not necessarily monogamous, family would be the natural corollary if this interpretation be accepted. But it need not apply in all cases. In several of the rare instances where the bodies have been carefully studied by physical anthropologists a marked discrepancy has been observed in the ages of the two corpses; in the Mesolithic burial from the Crimea, for instance, the male was forty to fifty years old, the female twenty to twenty-

---

[1] The European evidence is summarized by Maringer, "Menschenopfer im Bestattungsgebrauch Alteuropas," *Anthropos* (1942-5).

[2] *S.A.,* v. p. 162; Pequart, Boule, and Vallois, Institut de Paléont. hum., *Mem.* 18 (1937).

[3] Brunton, *The Badarian Civilization* (1928), p. 19.

[4] *Iraq,* ii, p. 39.

[5] *K.S.,* vii (1940), p. 92.

five. Such young females buried with mature males suggest concubines or slaves rather than wives. But even so, the practice does not indicate a high status for women, who would seem to have been treated as part of the personal property of the dead male.

But in practice the natural family seldom coincides with the institutional family, as it does with us. It is more often a larger unit, the matrilinear or patrilinear lineage or clan, that holds and transmits property and by the " blood feud " guarantees the security of the individual. To-day it assumes many forms, from the enlarged family in which two or three generations of the descendants of a single known ancestor keep together as a single household to the clan in which the ancestor may be mythical and the kinship between the clansmen more or less fictitious. Among the Iroquois and some other barbarian tribes clansmen sometimes—but not always—lived together under one roof as a single household in the literal sense. Soviet archæologists have therefore taken the large houses constructed in the Ukraine in Upper Palæolithic times and in Central Europe in some early Neolithic cultures as archæological indices of a clan organization, and their replacement by smaller dwellings in the later Neolithic of the latter area as indicative of the fission of the clan into economically autonomous natural families. They may well be right, but it does not follow that small houses, suitable for one natural family only, are incompatible with the existence of a clan organization.

Rather better evidence can be obtained from graves, at least where collective burial was practised. The large communal ossuaries of Early Minoan Crete and the gigantic megalithic tombs of Western and Northern Europe should most plausibly be regarded as clan sepulchres.

From kinship we naturally turn to property. Private property in weapons, tools, and ornaments used and worn by an individual is quite compatible with "primitive communism" and is recognized among even the simplest savages to-day. It seems attested archæologically even in Upper Palæolithic times by burial practices and "proprietary marks" engraved on bones and ivory weapons. But among such savages the hunting-grounds are generally "owned" by the clan collectively, and the proceeds of the chase are usually divided among all members of the group. While not demonstrable archæologically, this account probably holds good of the earlier prehistoric periods.

Of course, under simple economic conditions the articles thus owned by an individual were in most cases also made or collected by him or obtained by some simple form of exchange. They are in fact regarded as part of his personality and are quite naturally buried with him. Yet in time they acquire a value independent of their practical use and conferring status; they become wealth, and the accumulation becomes, if not an end in itself, at least a means to winning status in society. This transformation is naturally hard to recognize archæologically. But when weapons and ornaments are deposited as "votive offerings" in shrines or bogs, they are presumably already offered as wealth, and not as objects for use by the imaginary power or deity. Again, in stable societies i.e., in cultures that subsist for a considerable time—it has been repeatedly observed that the wealth of funerary furniture steadily declined even though the total wealth of the community was increasing.[1] That can plausibly be explained by the "greed of the heirs" when it was to their interest to acquire wealth.

Property in means of production is in a very different position. To barbarians this means primarily land and livestock. Among such tribes to-day land is generally col-

[1] Childe, "Directional Changes in Funerary Practices during 50,000 Years," *Man* (1945), No. 4.

lectively owned by the tribe, or at least the clan. It is often worked individually by families or households to whom plots are allotted for one season, or more rarely in perpetuity. But even in the last case, where the plot seems to a superficial observer to be " owned " by an individual proprietor, closer observation will reveal that quite a large proportion of the produce has to be distributed to relatives and clansmen.[1] But in the latter capacity the " proprietor " is himself entitled to receive portions of the produce from kinsmen's and clansmen's plots. The recognition of proprietary rights, such as that of buying and selling land like a commodity, results from a slow process in historical time. No archæological data that could even serve as a basis for discussion on the ownership of farmland are available till late in the Iron Age, when complete field systems can be examined.[2]

Ownership of flocks and herds would seem, from modern analogies, to pass more easily into private hands. The failure of Neolithic farmers to bury cattle or sheep with the deceased (apart from a joint of beef, mutton, or pork that might rank as mere provision for the journey) would imply that these domestic animals were not regarded in the same light as weapons and ornaments and were less personally owned. But by the Bronze Age literary evidence indicates that cattle were so easily alienated and exchanged that they served as a standard of value in Europe. And in the quite early " Amratian " culture of prehistoric Egypt models of cattle, deposited in graves, were presumably magic equivalents of real cattle and indicative of proprietary rights therein.

Finally, the archæological record bristles with documents illustrative of war, an institution that might contribute so

---

[1] Cf. Malinowski's chapter in *Coral Gardens.*
[2] Cf. Hatt, "The Ownership of Cultivated Land," K. Dansk. Vedens. Selsk., *Hist-phil. Meded.*, XXVI, No. 6 (Copenhagen; 1939).

much to the wealth of an individual person or group as to rank as economic or productive. Yet not all weapons were necessarily used for killing men; huntsmen use bows-and-arrows, slings, and spears, just as much as warriors do. Certain weapons of late Neolithic times, like "battle-axes" and still more rapiers and swords of bronze or iron, are admittedly instruments of war, though a well-known Mycenæan scene depicts a rapier being used in a lion-hunt. But even when weapons had demonstrably been used for homicide, as the arrow was in Mesolithic Brittany, it does not follow that the homicide was socially approved, still less that it was organized. Fortifications, on the other hand, can be distinguished from fences to keep out wild beasts, and must be regarded as intended for defence against attack by organized human foes—i.e., as instruments of war.

At the same time ethnography reveals—apart from murder, which is socially condemned—many varieties of approved homicide. Head-hunting is a recognized institution but often takes the form of the slaughter of an unsuspecting individual by an isolated hunter. That can hardly be termed war. Blood feuds may involve regular battles between families or clans within a single tribe or even in the same village. An archæologist could not hope to distinguish the results of such conflicts, the weapons used therein, or the defences built against them (as in Albania), from those correlative to conflicts between distinct political units. Moreover, ethnographers are agreed that wars are seldom waged between food-gathering or simple cultivating tribes for economic motives—the acquisition of hunting rights or of land for cultivation—but are indulged in by pastoralists and mixed farmers for the acquisition of cattle or slaves. Yet as a means of earning prestige or for other "uneconomic" reasons quite serious wars were undertaken by savages, notably in North America. After all, the speeches of Mussolini and Hitler would suffice to show that the absence of motives regarded by nineteenth-century Europeans as rational is no ground for denying the institutionalization of homicide on a large scale. Nevertheless, in prehistoric Europe positive evidences for warfare multiply only when the importance of stock-breeding in the rural economy increased. The correlation can hardly be altogether accidental.

CHAPTER VI

Culture Sequences in Savagery

In the light of the foregoing discussion let us survey the archæological record with a view to ascertaining whether the series of cultures, whose succession in time is established, reveal any general uniformities. We have already seen that savagery, barbarism, and civilization do in fact represent consecutive stages, at least in technological and economic development. Two further questions remain to be answered. Does archæology indicate the existence of institutions, or types of institution, common to and confined to cultures that precede in time those of the next main stage? In other words, what, if any, forms of social organization are common to all savage societies represented in the archæological record but which change with the transition from savagery to barbarism? Secondly, can we recognize, within savagery and within barbarism, subdivisions that everywhere succeed one another in the same order, just as savagery and barbarism do?

For convenience the archæological account of savagery can be examined from both these angles apart from barbarism. The best-known archæological representatives of this stage belong to the Palæolithic and Mesolithic stages in archæological classification. The former are undoubtedly older than any barbarian societies known or suspected. The latter may well be contemporary with some early stages of barbarism in other parts of the world, but these are generally so remote that influences from them may be ignored. Of course, food-gatherers have survived till to-day, and societies of such can be studied in the archæological as well as in the ethnographic record, but the archæological account is always less complete and little more reliable than the ethnographic.

Within the Palæolithic period, coinciding with the geological Pleistocene, and in the Mesolithic stage of the early Holocene prior to the emergence of the Neolithic economy of food-production in temperate Europe, well-defined culture sequences have been established. But while they certainly illustrate advances in technology and economy, they give very few and always inadequate indications of the nature of accompanying social changes. The Old Stone Age can easily be divided into two unequal but sharply contrasted periods—the Lower Palæolithic or Archæolithic of immense duration, perhaps of the order of 400,000 years, and the Upper Palæolithic or Miolithic that did not last even 100,000 years. The Lower Palæolithic can of course be subdivided both chronologically and into cultures, or rather culture cycles, but the only changes observable are technological. The surviving tools are made from stone—bone and antler were not yet shaped into implements—but, among some groups only, the technique of flaking stone improved, and more foresight was exercised in preparing the nodule or core. We can observe a somewhat gradual standardization of tools in respect of shape, and then a slight tendency to specialization of standardized tools. But even in the latest group recognized in Europe, the Mousterian, only two specialized forms—a blunt one-edged knife-scraper and a pointed two-edged knife—are really common.

Throughout this enormous period the only demonstrable sources of food remained hunting and collecting; there are no indications of fishing. No penetrating missile weapons are detectable; sharpened stakes may of course have been used as thrusting-spears, and in the last third of the period these may have been tipped with rather heavy triangular stone flakes.

The hunters sometimes lived in shallow caves, but the size of the group must have been quite small. No evidence survives as to its structure or as to the relations between groups. One child buried in a cave in Mt. Carmel[1] had been wounded by a sharp implement and Mousterians from Italy had certainly been killed by blows.[2] Cannibalism is attested both in the first third of the period in China[3] and in the last third in Europe—at Krapina in Croatia and Monte Ciceo in Italy.[2] The source of the victims is unknown, but the practice may have been dictated as much by superstition as by hunger. On the other hand, ritual burials survive from the last third. The deposition of implements and joints of meat in the grave has been reported in Europe, but the reliability of the reports has been questioned. One example from Mt. Carmel is, however, beyond dispute.

No Lower Palæolithic men whose skeletons survive are of modern type; all the extant skeletons are far more ape-like than those of any modern race. In particular the brain-case, even if not absolutely smaller, indicates an inferior development of several regions of the brain, notably the association areas. Yet there are some hints that even Palæanthropic men (fossil men not belonging to the species *Homo sapiens*) were right-handed and could communicate if not by articulate words at least by a very limited and rudimentary system of conventional symbols or signals. Similarly, the stone tools used by even the

[1] Garrod, McCown, and Bate, *The Stone Age of Mount Carmel* (Cambridge; 1937), pp. 95-8.

[2] Blanc, "I Paleontropi di Saccopastore e del Circeo," *Quartär*, IV (1942), p. 35.

[3] At Chou kou tien, Weidenreich, *Bulletin Geological Society of China*, XIX (1939), and "The Skull of *Sinanthropus pekinensis*," *Palæontologia Sinica*, D, 10, pp. 189 ff.

most backward of recent savages—the extinct Tasmanians —are technically more advanced than Lower Palæolithic implements. Hence no society observable by ethnographers can be regarded as systadial with or representative of any Lower Palæolithic culture.

In the succeeding Upper Palæolithic the number of distinguishable cultures is substantially multiplied, and all show an enormous technological advance over the latest Lower Palæolithic. A more economic but more sophisticated method of preparing flakes—the so-called blade technique—was generally employed. From blades a considerable variety of specialized and standardized tools—knives, scrapers, gravers, spoke-shaves, saws, awls, dart-heads— were manufactured. With their aid new materials—bone, ivory, and antler—were shaped to make tools : dart-heads, gorges, fish-spears, borers, needles, polishers, wedges, ornaments, and even sculptures.

Some sort of missile weapons tipped with penetrating points of flint, bone, or ivory were employed throughout the Upper Palæolithic. For their propulsion the bow was used quite early in North Africa and Spain.[1] North of the Alps and Pyrenees actual arrow-heads are not found till the early Holocene, by which time the flora and fauna of temperate Europe had come to resemble that of the Pleistocene of Spain, in which the bow had been used. During the steppe and tundra phase north of the Mediterranean the spear-thrower, still used in Australia and parts of America where the bow is unknown, is directly attested. In North America the spear-thrower preceded the bow by quite an appreciable archæological period.[2] But in Europe paintings in a recently discovered cave at Lascaux in the

[1] Caton Thompson, "The Aterian Industry" (Huxley Lecture), *J.R.A.I.* (1946), p. 2. Cf. Pericot, *La Cueva del Parpallo* (Madrid; 1942).

[2] Martin, Quimby, and Collier, *Indians Before Columbus* (Chicago; 1947).

Dordogne[1] belonging to an early phase of the Upper Palæolithic depict what seem to be arrows, sticking in game animals.

In any case, all Upper Palæolithic societies could use efficient missile weapons as well as traps in hunting. The location of settlements in at least some cases suggests battus or collective hunts. There are some indications of specialization in the pursuit of one particular kind of game. Ninety-nine per cent of the bones from a Croatian cave inhabited by Aurignacians belong to cave bear.[2] On Gravettian and Moravian camps in South Russia and Central Europe mammoth bones predominate; at Solutré in the Dordogne were remains of 100,000 horses; later reindeer bones predominate, though in art the bison is represented far more often than any other possible quarry.

Fishing[3] is attested from the beginning of the Upper Palæolithic, but at first only by fish-bones. Unambiguous fishing implements—gorges and spears—belong in Europe to the latest phase, the Magdalenian. Nets and fish-hooks are nowhere attested before the Holocene.

Upper Palæolithic hunters often lived or sheltered in caves, where such were available, but they could build huts or houses on the open steppe. The group that could live together would be larger than in the Lower Palæolithic. At Předmost no fewer than twenty skeletons were found together under stones and mammoth shoulder-blades. Whether or not deliberately buried, they are probably contemporary, but in no case need represent more than a fraction of the group. Finally, while no evidence is avail-

---

[1] Windels, *The Lascaux Cave Paintings* (1949), pp. 51-3. Unmistakable arrows and arrow-heads are also found on Hamburgian sites of the Upper Palæolithic in North Germany; cf. Rust, *Die altsteinzeitliche Renntierjägerlager Meiendorf* (1947).

[2] *Quartär*, I (1938), pp. 150-60.

[3] Clark, *Ant. J.*, XXVIII (1948), pp. 45-50.

able for land transport, it can confidently be asserted that some Upper Palæolithic societies had rafts that would cross the Straits of Gibraltar.

Relations between groups may perhaps be inferred from the distribution of materials. For instance, Mediterranean shells were somehow brought to Central France and to the Middle Dnieper. Specialization of labour is not detectable. But the masterly skill with which artists delineated animals in dark caves where they could never properly have seen their work implies a long and specialized training, though they were not necessarily full-time specialists.

The earliest artificial dwellings are small and perhaps rather temporary one-room huts (4.5 × 5.5 m. at Gagarino)[1] that would conveniently house a natural family. Later Soviet archæologists report more capacious structures that sound like a complex of the simpler huts under one roof. At Kostienki IV[2] there were eight hearths in a single long pit, 34 m. long and 5.6 m. wide, interpreted as a communal house of a clan. At Timonovka[3] dwellings 10 by 5 m. in area were grouped in pairs with allegedly only one hearth to each pair. Store-pits attached to each house would imply that stored food belonged in common to the whole household, which was certainly larger than the natural family.

Private property in weapons (darts and fish-spears) is indicated by " proprietary marks " engraved thereon, and in ornaments by their deposition in the grave.

Figurines of women, generally without faces but with the sexual attributes emphasized, have been taken as evidence of matriarchy and were in any case connected with

[1] Zamiatnin, "Gagarino," *Izvestia GAIMK* (1935).

[2] *S.A.*, v (1940), p. 279; cf. *K.S.*, iv (1940), p. 36, and Childe, *Antiquity* xxiv (1950), pp. 4-11.

[3] " Sotsialno-ekonomicheskiĭ stroĭ drevnikh obitateleĭ Timonovskĭ paleoliticheskoĭ stoyanki," *Sovietskaya Etnografia* (1935), p. 3.

some sort of fertility magic. A rather more plausible argument for matriarchy could be based on the burial of two youths with an old matron in one cave at Grimaldi[1] but would not of course be conclusive.

The most reliable evidence for differences of rank is the representation of a masked man in a dominating position in the cave of Trois Frères.[2] If he be rightly regarded as a professional sorcerer, that does not define his authority nor even mean that he was a full-time specialist.

Cannibalism was probably still practised ritually. A decapitated skeleton buried ceremonially in Wales, a skull cut for the extraction of the brain and then buried in a Derbyshire cave[3] and goblets made from human skulls[4] have been taken as evidences for head-hunting. Various kinds of hunting magic presumably inspired the celebrated Palæolithic art of central and western Europe. Offerings of first fruits are unambiguously attested at least for the end of the period; the reindeer-hunters who encamped at Meiendorf near Hamburg every year threw one reindeer weighted with stone into an adjoining mere.[5]

Some Palæolithic societies in Europe comprised talented and trained artists. Palæolithic art is normally naturalistic, but geometrical designs were also executed both in eastern and western Europe. In eastern Europe and in Spain a tendency is observable, in later phases, towards conventionalization, but elsewhere naturalism ruled till the end of the Pleistocene and beyond.

[1] Often described—e.g., Obermaier, *Fossil Man in Spain*; Boule, *Fossil Man*, fig. 201.

[2] Often illustrated—e.g., in Burkitt, *The Old Stone Age*.

[3] Described by L. A. Armstrong to the British Association, Section H, in 1948.

[4] Cf. Luquet, *L'art et la religion des hommes fossiles* (1926), pp. 171 ff. *Quartär*, IV, p. 163.

[5] Rust, *Meiendorf*, p. 110; *Die alt- und mittelsteinzeitlichen Funde von Stellmoor* (1943), p. 133.

The Mesolithic cultures of Europe[1] are all adaptations to a radically changed environment, but, apart from the appropriate adjustments, do not differ very dramatically from the Palæolithic. Yet the observable differences are highly significant. In all European Mesolithic societies great accumulations of shells—and in favourable circumstances of nuts—testify more positively to the economic importance of collecting. In all cases dogs, more or less domesticated, were presumably assisting men in the chase. The oldest fish-hooks and nets preserved anywhere were used by the Mesolithic denizens of the North European forests, conveniently termed Forest folk or Maglemoseans. These too have left us the earliest direct evidence on means of transport—paddles and a sledge-runner. Among the same people we find the oldest tolerably efficient kit of carpenter's tools—chisels, adzes, and gouges of stone or bone—and positive evidence for the bow drill, and pottery. This, the first artificial substance to be made by man, seems to have been invented somewhere near Denmark, but not before its use by the earlier Neolithic farmers of Hither Asia, though before there is any other indication of colonists from that quarter having reached northern Europe.[2] In fact the techniques of the two areas are quite distinct.

For trade the evidence from the Mesolithic stage is of the same sort as in the Palæolithic, though more frequent. Warfare is still only one of several possible deductions from the finding of a man pierced by an arrow. But headhunting has been plausibly inferred from a nest of skulls without trunks, buried under a layer of red ochre in the cave of Offnet in Bavaria; out of thirty-three of these, twenty were of women and nine of children, thus recalling

---

[1] Summary in Childe, *Dawn*, Chap. I.

[2] " The Culture Sequence in Northern Europe " in *Annual Report University of London Institute of Archæology*, 4 (1946-7).

the sort of booty an Oceanian head-hunting expedition would like to secure without an open battle. Cannibalism is still attested.[1]

No female figurines survive to suggest a high status for women. Double burials from the Crimea and Morbihan[2] may, as I have already remarked, point in the opposite direction. The cemetery of Teviec shows that some individuals were accorded higher honours at burial than the rest. But there were only a dozen graves in all, and only three were thus distinguished. Their occupants enjoyed peculiar prestige, but we have no idea from what it was derived or what prerogatives it conferred. Hereditary chieftainship would certainly be a very premature assumption.

The Mesolithic Age lasted a long time—in northern Europe probably 5000 years, or as long as the whole of recorded history. Naturally sequences of cultures can be distinguished in it, but in most cases their constituents differ from one another only in peculiarities of flint work. Only on the North European plain are the changes more comprehensive and illuminating, but there they are partly explicable by reference to the environment, since the distribution of land and sea, the climate, and the composition of the forests altered substantially during the period. Apart from general adaptations to these changes in environment, some common tendencies may be rather precariously inferred during the three phases into which the Mesolithic can be divided. There is a tendency to multiplication of distinguishable cultures, due largely to divergent specialization in adaptation to varying local conditions or to the pursuit of particular kinds of game, but accentuated by the isolation consequent upon the flooding of the North Sea

[1] Degerbol in Mathiassen, etc., "Bopladsen Dyrholmen," K. Dansk. Videns. Selskab. *Ark-kunsthist. Skrifter*, I, 1 (Copenhagen; 1942), pp. 118 ff.

[2] I.P.H. *Mem.* 18 (1937); see note 2, p. 43.

and Baltic depressions and also by contact with peoples with quite independent cultural traditions. There is perhaps a growing emphasis on fishing, accompanied in some groups by increasingly sedentary habits. In Phase I we know only summer camps of reindeer hunters who had travelled perhaps considerable distances from their unknown winter quarters. In Phase II also we know best temporary summer encampments, devoted, however, to fishing and fowling as well as to hunting and collecting. In Phase III, while some societies maintained this semi-nomadic life, some groups settled down to a more sedentary life near convenient oyster-banks on sheltered stretches of the coast. It was at first only the last-named, the so-called Ertebølle folk, who used pottery.

These hunter-fisher cultures persisted, after the advent of the first farmers, for some time in Denmark and southern Sweden, much longer east of the Baltic. These epimesolithic[1] or opsimiolithic savages maintained the old culture and much of the old equipment unaltered, save for the addition of pottery in most areas. Changes in ceramic styles do indeed define a chronological sequence of cultures, but no general sociological changes can be detected at present. On the other hand, taken as a stadial whole the opsimiolithic societies of the East Baltic and central Russia give some significant sociological information about savage societies of an undeniably high antiquity and probably still very little modified by contact with food-producing barbarians.

Cemeteries of eighty (Gotland)[2] to one hundred and fifty (L. Onega)[3] graves show that in favourable circum-

---

[1] *Epimesolithic*: term applied to cultures which preserve the mesolithic economy (hunting, fishing, and collecting) in Neolithic times and exhibit some traits, such as polished axes or pottery, normally associated with Neolithic cultures.

[2] *Acta Arch.*, X (1939), pp. 61 ff.

[3] *S.A.*, VI (1940), pp. 46-62.

stances quite large communities of hunter-fishers could live on a territory small enough to allow all their members to use a common burial-ground and probably to live part of each year at least in the same encampment—for on Gotland the graves were dug in or between the dwellings of the living. Among the 150 graves excavated on Olenii Ostrov in L. Onega, double graves of man and woman buried simultaneously were "not uncommon"; in one, two women were buried with the man. This certainly encourages the belief that such graves represent some sort of *sati,* but is a warning against their interpretation as evidences of monogamy. On the other hand, figurines, not very clearly sexed but more probably female than male, were used as in the Palæolithic. Five graves were exceptionally elaborate, containing male skeletons buried erect in a deep pit. These must have been outstanding personalities. One was accompanied with such rich gear as undeniably to deserve the title "chief" (*vozhd*) given him by the Russian excavators.

I shall complete this account of Old World savages by summarizing the sequence of cultures, at first closely related to those just described, in the forest zone of Siberia round L. Baikal, as defined by Okladnikov[1] in 1938. In the first or Izakovo stage, hunting with bow and arrows and throwing spear was the basis of life. The dead of both sexes were buried extended with their arms or implements, ornaments, and pots. In the succeeding or Serovo culture fishing implements also are found, but hunting still makes the more important contribution. The great reinforced or Mongolian bow is used. Bows are buried even in the graves of women, who may be accompanied by the bodies of young children. Then in the Kitoï culture fishing begins to be more important than hunting; fish-hooks, but no bows, are buried in the graves, and there is

[1] *Vestnik Drevneĭ Istoriĭ,* 1 (1938), pp. 246-56.

marked diversity in the wealth of their furniture. At least one grave was so exceptionally richly furnished that its occupant might almost have been some kind of chief. Materials not occurring in nature locally now give the first indications of some sort of trade. In several graves the corpses of women accompany the male skeletons—*sati*. Finally in the Glazzkovo stage fishing has become the principal means of support. Objects of copper, derived perhaps by trade, along with other imports, from the farmers of the steppes, were not very regularly obtained. But war is now attested by weapons and even bone splint armour. Poor and rich graves are contrasted. In some rich graves lies a second skeleton without grave-gear, presumably therefore a slave. One rich grave[1] contained a man and a woman with an infant in her arms. She was as richly dressed as her consort but had been shot to death with arrows. My Russian colleagues accept this as evidence for *sati* and a patriarchal family in savagery.

So the archæological record is found to be regrettably but not surprisingly deficient in indications of the social organization or lack of it in Lower Palæolithic hordes. From the scraps available no generalizations are permissible. In the Upper Palæolithic and Mesolithic the record, where fuller, is also one-sided. It offers a clear picture of nothing more than the economy and material culture adapted to the peculiar environments of Ice Age Europe and of the northern forest zone in early post-glacial times. That does not afford a basis for generalization even on the development of technology within a food-gathering economy. Even less could the very scanty sociological inferences possible justify inductions as to the institutions and forms of social organization proper to savagery in general.

It is, however, plain that head-hunting, cannibalism,

[1] *K.S.*, VII (1940), pp. 90-3; cf. IX (1941), pp. 6-14.

some kind of magic, and even offerings of first fruits were already practised by some savages who could not have been exposed to the " corrupting " influences of materially more advanced societies. And on the evidence of double graves even such savage women might be subjected to the dominance of males as much as were their barbarian and civilized sisters.

Finally, the Epimesolithic cemetery on L. Onega proves the existence of some sort of chieftainship among savages who are not very likely to have been seriously corrupted by contact with barbarian farmers. This evidence admittedly belongs to a chronologically late epoch, but not to a stage that can be clearly recognized as technically much more advanced than the Mesolithic level.

CHAPTER VII

Culture Sequences in Barbarism : (1) *Temperate Europe*

The thorough and systematic examination of the prehistoric monuments and relics in several provinces of the
temperate forest zone of Europe[1] has resulted in the recognition of well-defined sequences of cultural periods. These
sequences are most complete in Central Europe, Denmark
with southern Sweden, Lowland England, and Highland
Britain, but the number of periods distinguishable in each
province varies. In most periods in each sequence there is
sufficient evidence for a fairly adequate characterization of
the productive system and economy and some hints as to
the scale and form of social organization. By comparison
it will be possible to define stages at least in technological
and economic development represented more or less accurately throughout the zone. But the correspondence between the stages in the four provinces named will be found
to be far from exact.

These discrepancies are not surprising; for the four provinces represent somewhat different environments. All
indeed lie within the zone of evenly distributed annual
rainfall, and all would naturally be covered with continuous forest, but soils and climates differ. Central Europe
here means primarily the löss lands of the basins of the
Middle and Upper Danube, the Vistula, the Oder, the
Elbe, and the Rhine. The löss offers an ideal soil for cultivation with even very primitive tools and supports a

[1] For general information see Childe, *Dawn of European Civilization* (1950), Chaps. VII-X and XVI-XVIII.

87

deciduous forest. The climate is rather continental, with hot summers and cold, but not extreme, winters. Northern Europe is covered with moraines providing variable soils, on the poorer of which only conifers thrive. Owing to the higher latitude, the mean annual temperature is lower than that farther south, but thanks to the moderating effect of the sea the winter cold is hardly more extreme than in the Upper Danube basin. Finally, in Britain as an island the climate is in general mild and oceanic with a tendency to excessive rainfall most marked in the Highland Zone. In the Lowland Zone of England some of the most fertile soil is clay unsuitable for cultivation with primitive equipment, but extensive chalk uplands and limestone outcrops offered soils as attractive in their way as the Central European löss. The Highland Zone, including Cornwall, Wales, the northern English counties, and Scotland, is not only rugged and mountainous but composed of ancient rocks that are liable to yield acid, unfertile soils save where capped by recent moraines.

It will be convenient to begin with a summary description of the most relevant features of the successive cultural periods in one typical province, and only then to rearrange the material in a more schematic stadial form. Let us take the löss lands of Central Europe[1] with special reference to the Upper Danube basin.

In Danubian Period I the rural economy was based on the cultivation of wheat and barley in small plots, tilled with hoes. These plots were abandoned as soon as exhausted. Their cultivation was always combined with the breeding of cattle, pigs, and a few sheep or goats. Yet animal husbandry seems to have played a subordinate role, and the deciduous forest, while congenial to cows and

[1] For the Neolithic stages fuller details are given by Butter, *Die donauländische und westische Kulturkreis der jüngeren Steinzeit* (Berlin; 1938); for the Bronze Age in Childe, *The Danube in Prehistory* (Oxford; 1929).

pigs, did not favour the expansion of flocks.[1] The contribution of hunting to the food supply seems to have been negligible. Transport and communications were effected by waterways. There is no evidence for industrial specialization within or between communities which could make all essential equipment from local materials. Nevertheless, choice stones for querns and adzes were occasionally transported for a hundred miles or so, and even pots were conveyed as much as fifty miles from the place of manufacture. Finally, in addition to this intermittent and irregular short distance "trade," shells of *Spondylus gaederopi* for use as ornaments and charms were imported from the Mediterranean.

The known settlements seem to have been hamlets of some thirteen (or possibly twice as many) houses.[2] Some of these are so large—as much as 90 feet long and 20 feet wide—that they could house a clan rather than a single natural family. Grain was stored in granaries, but the relation of these to the dwellings does not permit of any assertion as to the proprietary rights of households over the stored grain. No building stands out as a chieftain's residence, nor do grave furnitures point to differences in rank. Female figures were moulded in clay or depicted on pottery vases. No edifices have been found that could be regarded as temples. Weapons of war are conspicuously absent.

In Period II the rural economy seems better balanced owing to increased reliance on animal husbandry. Moreover, the natural resources in wild food were exploited, since bones of game-animals and weapons of the chase— or perhaps of war—occur in settlements. "Trade" diffused some materials such as Hungarian obsidian as much

[1] Clark, "Sheep and Swine in the Husbandry of Prehistoric Europe," *Antiquity*, XXI (1947), pp. 122-37.

[2] Buttler's reconstructions are probably wrong; cf. Paret, *Germania*, XXVI (1942), pp. 84-103; Childe, *P.P.S.*, XV (1949), pp. 77 ff.

as 300 miles from its natural source, but still only occasionally and in small quantities.

The size of settlements can be deduced from cemeteries of sixty-five to eighty graves[1] and a hamlet of twenty-three houses.[2] All the known houses of the period are of modest size, some 30 feet long by 18 feet broad, suitable to a natural family. None looks like a chief's palace nor do any graves in the cemeteries stand out as " royal tombs." In one cemetery two double graves, in which one corpse was accompanied by rich offerings and the other by hardly any, might be taken as indicating the ownership and immolation of slaves.[1] In several instances men and women were buried together.[1] If that be evidence for a patriarchal family, female figurines, which are commoner than in Period I, could just as well be cited as indicators of matriarchy. Models of animals, birds, and houses were also made, but none of phalli or male personages.

Some settlements are fortified, and this, combined with the occurrence of weapons, proves the practice of war. At the same time, in Period II prehistorians can recognize a number of cultures, all probably sharing the foregoing characters but displaying divergent traditions in pottery, domestic architecture, ornaments, and even burial rites.

In Period III we observe a still further multiplication of cultures. In general the emphasis in rural economy shifts from corn-growing to stock-breeding and hunting, but not to the same extent in all societies. Indeed, one could now speak of a " separation of pastoral tribes from the mass of agricultural barbarians," provided we remember that even the " pastoral tribes " also cultivated cereals. Flocks of sheep also multiplied[3] so as to provide wool for

----

[1] E.g., at Zengovarkony, *Archæologia Hungarica,* XXIII (1939).

[2] Aichbühl, Reinerth, *Das Federseemoor als Siedelungsland der Vorzeitmensch* (Augsburg; 1929).

[3] Notably in the so-called Baden culture, as at Ossarn in Lower Austria.

a domestic textile industry. On the other hand, there are hints that among some societies plough cultivation of fields was beginning to supersede the tillage of plots with hoes.[1] It must be insisted that pastoralism meant at this period in temperate Europe primarily the breeding of cattle and pigs, and that this sort of stock-raising is no more, but perhaps less, compatible with nomadism than corn-growing by the slash-and-burn method. Again, an increase in the proportion of wild as compared with domestic animals eaten betokens a more complete exploitation of natural resources, perhaps even a more economical treatment of herds, but in no case a " relapse " towards savagery.[2]

Horses were now included among the domestic stock and were in all probability used for transport. They may have been harnessed to sleds, which had been known in the forest zone since Mesolithic times, but there is as yet no evidence for wheeled vehicles.

The known industries could still be carried on without specialization of labour within the community, but inter-communal specialization must be inferred from the discovery of axe-factories where rock of superior quality cropped out and from an incipient use of copper, which was presumably collected, and possibly mined and even smelted, by groups of at least part-time specialists. Some villages on the Austrian lakes may indeed have supplemented local food supplies by the proceeds of trade in copper, which could be shipped down rivers from these lakes, and the authors of one archæological culture—the so-called Beaker-folk—are thought to have lived largely by trade. In any case the interchange of products between

[1] In Holland plough-furrows have been observed in the soil under a "Beaker" barrow belonging in time to Period III or IV. Van Giffen, "Grafheuvels te Zwaagdijk," *West-Friesland Oud en Nieuw,* XVII Drenthe, 1944.

[2] Cf. Krichevskiï, "Indogermanskiï Vopros," *Izvestia GAIMK.,* 100 (1933).

regions was more frequent than before, though still too irregular to deserve the description of regular trade. At the same time warlike intercourse may be deduced from the prominence of weapons of war, while all known settlements were fortified either naturally or artificially.

Several cultures of Period III are known only from graves. The cemeteries thus formed do not seem to comprise more than sixty graves. On the other hand, villages may consist of as many as fifty—small—houses or huts.[1] Nothing like a chieftain's residence has been detected in any village, but among one of the more pastoral societies[2] burials in mortuary houses under barrows may possibly be regarded as those of chiefs.

Burials of a man and a woman in the same grave still occur, and there are now no longer female figurines to be claimed as indications of matriarchy; their place is sometimes taken by models of bulls and rams. Indeed, Period III witnesses the emergence of a warlike, pastoral, and very probably patriarchal regime, but certainly not any division of society into classes.

Period IV coincides with the first, "Early," phase of the local Bronze Age, but is distinguished from III not by any radical change in the rural economy but by the establishment of regular trade and, as a result, the use of metal for weapons, ornaments, and craftsmen's tools. That presup poses the existence of full-time specialists, but these were apparently itinerant merchant-artificers rather than resident members of the local groups. The distribution of metal within Central Europe seems at this time to have been bound up with trade in other materials, of which amber is most easily recognized in the archæological record.

[1] "Altheim" settlement on Goldberg, *Germania*, XXI (1937), pp. 149-58; Homolka, Bohemia, *Proc. American Phil. Soc.*, LXXI (1932), pp. 384-5.
[2] At the Baalberg in Central Germany and in the "Battle-Axe" culture, *Offa*, I (1936), pp. 77-82.

Now the amber trade at least was demonstrably "international." Some of the fossil resin, collected ultimately in Jutland and Samland, found a market in civilized States in Crete and Greece, while in return some manufactures of civilization, albeit only beads, reached barbarians in Central Europe. For by Period IV of Danubian barbarism Mediterranean societies had already achieved civilization. Hence it is arguable that the capital needed for the development of regular commerce and a metallurgical industry in temperate Europe was derived in part at least from the social surplus accumulated in civilized States in the East Mediterranean. But in Period IV metal was still scarce and costly north of the Alps and was used mainly for weapons and ornaments, and that only by societies living on the main trade routes that naturally followed river valleys. The more pastoral tribes, inhabiting the intervening uplands, remained on the whole Neolithic.

No settlements are known in Period IV save along the Tisza, but the cemeteries may now comprise over 100 graves.[1] In them no chieftains' graves are recognizable, but men and women might still be buried together. Only in the Saale valley, rich in salt and ore, and a junction of several trade routes, do a few burials in mortuary houses, under great barrows, and accompanied by rich grave gear, and apparently by human victims, stand out as isolated evidences of the institution of divine kingship in one special society. And these kings founded no lasting dynasties.

Period V is distinguished by the more general use of metal among the pastoralists as well as among the lowland cultivators.

During Period VI rural economy and industry underwent a transformation. At length plough agriculture took the place of plot cultivation, and slash-and-burn made way

---

[1] At Polepy, Bohemia, 141 graves, Dvořak, *Pamatky Archeol.*, XXXV (1926-7), pp. 31-44.

for an alternation between crop and fallow. Sheep could graze on the stubble and fallow fields, so that flocks increased substantially.[1]

Transport was now demonstrably accelerated by the use of wheeled vehicles, which, in the form of horse-drawn chariots, served also as engines of war. Metal tools were used not only for fine work by craftsmen but also by farmers for clearing forests and reaping, and by miners for breaking up ore.

Accordingly there must have been resident bronze-smiths in most communities, and probably a few other specialists. On the other hand, quite substantial communities, composed largely of full-time specialists, must have been engaged in the extraction of salt, metals, and perhaps other materials. In the eastern Alps actual salt-mines and copper-mines with roasters and smelters have been discovered.[2] The Mitterberg main lode, it can be calculated, employed continuously some 180 workers, yielded an annual output of about 20 tons of copper, and consumed every year for the smelters alone the wood from nineteen acres of forest, without including that required for timbering mine-shafts and galleries.

Regular trade secured the distribution of raw materials and of finished articles, such as bronze cups, cauldrons, and helmets, all over the province, and Danubian manufactures reached the Ukraine, Scandinavia, Britain, and Italy.[3] Commerce with civilized Mediterranean societies is attested at the beginning of the period best by amber,

[1] See note 1, p. 89.

[2] See Ebert's *Reallexikon, I,* s.v. Bergbau and Pittioni, in *Man* 1948, p. 121.

[3] Cf., especially, Sprockhoff, "Handelsgeschichte der germanischen Bronzezeit" (*Vorgeschichtliche Forschungen,* 7) (1930); Holste, "Der frühhallstattzeiltliche Gefässfunde von Ehingen," *Praehistorica,* 5 (Vienna; 1939); von Merhart, "Zu den ersten Metallhelmen Europas," *BRGK.,* xxx (1941); Childe, "The Final Bronze Age in the Near East and in Temperate Europe," *P.P.S.* xiv (1948).

as earlier in Mycenæan Greece, but before the close of Period VI it found a civilized market nearer at hand in the Greek colonies and the Etruscan cities of the Apennine peninsula.

Such active trade required the social recognition of conventional standards of measurement. Lead weights[1] actually surviving show that standards previously sanctioned among the civilized societies of the East Mediterranean were now accepted, among the traders at least, in barbarian Europe. Gold rings may have served as media of exchange. The use of such standards of value is symptomatic of a new conception of wealth.

On the other hand, war is still more prominent in the archæological record. Most settlements were strongly fortified; swords are among the most conspicuous products of the bronze-smiths. These metal weapons, and still more shields and helmets of beaten bronze, must, however, have been very costly. War chariots fashioned by expert wainwrights and drawn by specially trained steeds must have been available only to a few persons who could accumulate the still rather exiguous social surplus. Hence chieftainship, reinforced as in Mycenæan Greece by monopoly of decisive armament as well as economic power, is to be expected.

A settlement at Buchau[2] on the Federsee in Wurtemberg consisted at first of thirty-eight small huts, but a later settlement on the same site consisted of a group of nine large farm-houses. Each of the later steadings comprised a stable and a granary, at last supplying indisputable evidence, confirmed elsewhere, of the stalling of cattle and of the existence of private property in livestock and in the produce of fields. Better evidence for the enlargement of the unit of settlements is afforded by cremation cemeteries

[1] Dechelette, *Manuel d'Archéologie*, Vol. II, part I, p. 401.
[2] See note 2, p. 88.

(often termed urnfields) comprising from 200 to 400 graves.[1]

Burials in urnfields are generally poorly furnished with gear. This may mean that possessions such as weapons and bronze vessels were now regarded as heritable wealth rather than as a personal extension of their owner's person. A few somewhat richer graves may be accepted as those of chieftains, especially as in contemporary settlements, like Buchau, one house rather larger and more commodious than the rest can be safely attributed to a village headman. Unlike the " royal tombs " of Periods III, IV, and VII in Greece, Egypt, and Mesopotamia, these tombs and dwellings differ only in degree but not in kind from those of " commoners." Of kings enjoying more than strictly local authority there is still no trace.

Burials, being after cremation, afford no good evidence as to the position of women and the existence of slaves. Labour in the extractive industries was undoubtedly organized and articulated, but there is no evidence as to whether it was servile.

No Late Bronze Age temples are known. Portable ritual objects and charms were used and buried in graves, and some of the best attested cases of cannibalism[2] come from Bohemia in Danubian VI.

Danubian VII coincides with the First Iron Age or Hallstatt period of archæological terminology. It is distinguished from Period VI in the first instance by the general use of iron in place of bronze for tools and for some weapons. Iron ores being much commoner than those of copper and tin, metal tools were now cheaper than before, and were available for more extensive clear-

---

[1] Over 300 at Kelheim, Bavaria (Kimmig, " Die Urnenfelderkultur in Baden," *Römisch-german. Forschungen*, XIV (1941)), and 221 excavated, 400 estimated, at Zagyvarpálfalva, North Hungary, *Arch. Ertésitö*, XLIII (1929), p. 35.

[2] Childe, *Danube*, p. 344.

ance and drainage operations, so opening up more land for cultivation and grazing.

No general expansion of secondary industry followed, but new extractive industries developed, notably round the iron ores of Moravia, Silesia, western Germany, and Lorraine. The metal was transported as ingots[1] in a form recognized as standard also by the civilized Assyrians. Though iron ore is so common that many communities could have supplied themselves with metal, trade within Central Europe did not apparently fall below the level attained in Danubian VI.

On the other hand, the second decisive peculiarity of Period VII is due to the proximity of civilized markets. Not only were the Greek colonies and Etruscan States in central Italy purchasers of barbarian products—metals, salt, slaves—but about 600 B.C. this civilized market was brought to the very edge of the temperate zone by the Etruscan annexation of the Po valley and the foundation of a Greek colony—Massilia—at Marseilles. As a result an increasing stream of civilized " luxuries "—metal-ware, Attic vases, wine—flowed across the Alps.[2] In their train came at length a purely conventional standard of value and medium of exchange—money—not in the form of coins but of spits,[3] such as were current among the Etruscans and earlier among the Greeks.

A third innovation distinguishing Period VII was the use of the horse for riding.[4] This accelerated communications and revolutionized warfare. The new arm—cavalry

[1] *Real*. III, s.v. Eisen.

[2] Jacobsthal, *Germania*, XVIII (1934), p. 17; Jacobsthal and Langsdorf, *Die Bronzeschnabelkannen* (Berlin; 1939); de Navarro, *Antiquity*, II, pp. 425-37.

[3] Dechelette, *Manuel*, II, pp. 1390, 1558.

[4] Wiesner, "Fahren und Reiten in Alteuropa," *Der alte Orient*, XXXVIII (1949); Hermes, *Anthropos* XXXII (1937), pp. 113-42.

—must have been far more efficient than chariotry in a wooded and accidented terrain.

A very substantial expansion of population is deducible from cemeteries[1] that may now comprise over 1000 graves and from settlements[2] covering 12 acres or more and girt with enormous fortifications. In practice two types of settlement might be distinguished. In addition to the large fortresses—townships or oppida (fortified tribal refuges, generally on hill tops)—just mentioned, are numerous smaller fortified areas covering 5 acres or so, obviously villages or hamlets. One of the latter class, the Goldberg,[3] contained about a dozen farm-houses, each with stable and granary, and a large timber hall in a strongly fortified inner enceinte, evidently the castle of the local chief. In the great fortified oppida we might expect the palace of a high chief or king.

The funerary record confirms this expectation. In many cemeteries excavation discloses three grades of interments[4] —the majority (poorly furnished and generally after cremation) under small barrows; a much smaller number of extended skeletons, accompanied, if male, by swords and other accoutrements but always by rich gear, under large barrows; a very few shaft graves or mortuary houses under huge barrows and containing the body of a warrior buried in a four-wheeled hearse and accompanied by the trappings of a warhorse, treasures of precious metal, and Mediterranean imports.[5] These royal tombs thus provide

[1] E.g., Iddelsfelder Haardt on the Rhine.

[2] E.g., 12 acres for the Hueneburg, Upflamör, Würtemberg, *Real.,* III, p. 248.

[3] Goldberg in Würtemberg, Bersu, " Vorgeschichtliche Siedelungen auf dem Goldberg bei Nördlingen," *Deutschtum und Ausland,* Heft 23/4.

[4] Dvořak, *Knížeci Pohrby na Vozech* (Praha; 1938).

[5] Paret, " Das ürstengrab der Hallstattzeit von Bad-Cannstatt," Anhang zu *Fundberichte aus Schwaben,* N.F. VIII (1935).

the first conclusive evidence for the effective political unification of local communities into still tiny kingdoms.

Period VIII—the Second Iron Age, often designated La Tène[1]—reveals the outcome of tendencies already operative in Hallstatt times. Farming has been made more productive by metal ploughshares and other improvements in equipment and by technical advances such as the provision of fodder for stalled cattle.

The surplus productible now suffices to support quite a variety of specialized craftsmen who can manufacture labour-saving devices such as rotary querns.[2] Many centres of population were large enough to make it possible for specialists to produce pottery *en masse* on the wheel, instead of leaving the individual housewives to build up their own pots tediously by hand. Artist craftsmen wandered from court to court, producing triumphs of metalwork in which Classical forms and motives were adapted to barbarian tastes.[3]

Trade both among the barbarians and between them and the civilizations of Greece and Rome continued to expand. Greek coins were first accepted as currency and then imitated among barbarian tribes who began to issue their own coinages.

Military tactics were transformed at the beginning of the period by the adoption from the Etruscans of an improved chariot, lighter but presumably more solid than the Late Bronze Age forms. In the sequel missile weapons, notably slings, were effectively developed.

At first royal tombs are more conspicuous and magnificent than ever, but they are confined to the very beginning of the period and to the valleys of the Rhine and the

[1] The best general account is still that of Dechelette, *op. cit.* Cf. also, Vouga, *La Tène*.

[2] Childe, *Antiquity*, xvii (1943).

[3] Jacobsthal, *Early Celtic Art* (Oxford; 1944).

Upper Danube. More common even in the early La Tène phase are cemeteries that include a minority of chariot graves. The latter, though richly furnished, seem too numerous—there were seventy-four at Thuizy on the Marne—to be called "royal tombs." They certainly belong to a ruling class, but monarchy was giving way to aristocracy. Cæsar's account, of course, confirms this. From his period not even chariot burials are known. Indeed, the richest pre-conquest La Tène burial[1] seems to be that of a carpenter, and attests the high social status attainable by a skilled craftsman.

Among the seventy-four chariot burials at Thuizy[2] no fewer than twenty-eight contained the skeleton of a woman (some, but not most, comparatively young) as well as of a man. Evidences for *sati* are available at other cemeteries. Similarly gang-chains now afford direct and unimpeachable evidence for slavery. Finally, some small shrines were erected in late La Tène times, but there is no indication that they were on the way to becoming centres for the accumulation of wealth comparable to those of Babylonia or the courts of divine kings.

For all their area and despite the specialist craftsmen working in them, the La Tène oppida probably remained townships inhabited mainly by working farmers rather than cities in the Mediterranean sense. The latter were imposed on temperate Europe by the Romans after military conquest. Similarly, despite close intercourse with literate Etruscans, Greeks, and Romans, the barbarians of the La Tène period have left no documents to show that they adopted writing for any practical purpose. On the criterion here adopted they never achieved civilization for

---

[1] Celles, Dechelette, *Manuel*, II, part 3 (1944), p. 1051.
[2] Fordrignier, " Sur les speultures doubles," *Bull. Soc. Anthr.*, Paris (1880), pp. 320-7.

themselves; for literacy as well as urban life was introduced by the Roman conquerors.

By way of comparison let us survey still more cursorily
the record of prehistoric England.[1]

The first period is dominated by a Neolithic economy
that diverges from that of Danubian I first by a greater
emphasis on the breeding of cattle, pigs, and sheep, though
still with little attention to hunting; secondly by the existence of communities of flint-miners who must have been
at least part-time specialists; thirdly by the display of warlike traits—an abundance of arrow-heads and the fortification of "camps" on hilltops; fourthly by the manufacture
of phalli, in addition to rare female figurines. It is doubtful whether the hilltop camps were permanently inhabited;
only a couple of isolated Neolithic houses have been identified. Some of the dead were buried under monumental
long-barrows, but it is uncertain whether these were family
vaults for chiefly families or communal ossuaries. In any
case the practice of collective burial has robbed us of the
usual "evidence" as to marital usages.

Period II in England, dominated by the Beaker culture,
could be compared most closely to Danubian III, especially in its rural economy, which is distinctly of the
"pastoral" type as defined for Central Europe (p. 90).
But no hint of the use of a plough, nor of the domestication of horses, has yet come to light. On the other hand,
the Beaker culture is traditionally assigned to the "Early
Bronze Age," and this terminology is justified inasmuch
as metal was used for weapons and ornaments, and trade
was more regular and extensive than would be compatible
with Neolithic self-sufficiency. Moreover, the Beaker-folk
inaugurated the erection of monumental "sanctuaries"—
circles of huge stones or enormous posts—that presupposed

[1] Childe, *Prehistoric Communities of the British Isles* (Edinburgh;
1948).

the co-operation and the ritual, if not political, unification of all the inhabitants of areas so extensive as Salisbury Plain and the North Wiltshire-Berkshire Downs. Silbury Hill may conceivably cover the remains of a "divine king" of the latter region, but he, if he existed, founded no dynasty, and no other unambiguous evidence for chieftainship is provided by funerary record, while Beaker settlements are quite unknown. Double graves of man and woman,[1] and cases of cannibalism[2] have been reported. Still only five per cent of the Beaker folk known were rich enough to be buried with any metal objects!

In the third main cultural period such social unity as may be denoted by the universal dominance of Beaker-folk (these were really far from a homogeneous group) breaks up. The economy became still more markedly pastoral, and no trace of anything resembling a village has been discovered. On the other hand, trade was regularized on the same lines as in Central Europe, and metalware was widely distributed by itinerant merchant artificers. As in Danubian IV and V this commerce was international; British or Irish manufactures reached Scandinavia and Central Europe on the one hand and Crete on the other, while in return Baltic amber and Aegean fayence beads were brought to Britain.

On the superb pastures of the Wessex Downs a hundred barrows covering richly furnished graves would seem to belong to an aristocracy of petty chieftains. Similar graves occur in Cornwall and more sparsely in other parts of Lowland England; only a dozen are known from the whole of Scotland.

English III coincides in time with the latter half of Danubian IV and the whole of V and the Late Minoan and Mycenæan period in Greece after 1500 B.C. But it

[1] E.g., Abercromby, *Bronze Age Pottery* (1912), I, p. 71.
[2] E.g., Mortimer, *Forty Years Digging,* p. 24.

must overlap with the Late Bronze Age of Central Europe.

That phase is represented by English IV, but only in the south of England. There, as in Central Europe, plough cultivation replaced slash-and-burn, with the same consequences for the whole rural economy. Even earlier the metallurgical industries had undergone the same sort of revolutionary expansion as on the Continent, but this affected the whole of the British Isles.

On the other hand, no village settlements are known in England but only lone steadings and cattle-kraals, and there is as yet no evidence of wheeled carts or chariots, nor of chieftains.

Period V in southern England is distinguished only by the introduction of iron tools, with some consequent expansion of agriculture. Settlements are represented by small open villages (none completely excavated) and large isolated farms. All seem to have been mainly self-sufficing. There are no indications of extensive unification, whether politically under chiefs or economically through intensified commerce; trade, in fact, markedly declined.

Period VI witnesses the gradual establishment of a rather impoverished version of the La Tène culture through a series of invasions at first led by charioteers from the Marne. The most typical settlements are now strongly fortified villages. All are smaller than Continental oppida—10 to 24 acres is the normal area, 60 acres quite exceptional—and comprised fewer specialist craftsmen. Professional potters did not set up their wheels in England, but artist craftsmen presumably found patrons in petty chieftains. The latter are known directly from a few chariot burials—a dozen in eastern Yorkshire and a couple elsewhere. Coined money was not used, but bars of iron were accepted as currency.

Finally, in the first century B.C. an invasion of Belgic Gauls introduced a heavy plough with which it was possible for the first time to exploit the heavier but more fertile soils of south-eastern England. The Belgæ established small monarchical States whose princes issued coined money to take the place of currency bars. But even their capital at Camulodunum (Colchester) fell far short of being a city. In Britain, as on the Continent, civilization—urban and literary—was imposed by the Romans.

Northern Europe

Finally, in Denmark and southern Sweden[1] a sequence of nine cultural periods of barbarism down to the beginning of the Christian era provides a useful comparison with the Danubian and the British, even though it does not take us down to the dawn of civilization in the north. The first three periods, all divisions of the local Neolithic Age though of considerable duration and easily defined by changes of fashion in funerary architecture, weapon types, and ceramic decoration, exhibit no recognizable divergences in economy and social organization, so that Northern I, II, and III may be bracketed together; IV and V can be similarly amalgamated for the present purpose. On the other hand, in Periods II and III certainly, and possibly even in I, two quite distinct Neolithic societies can be recognized with contrasted economies, and both were juxtaposed during Periods I and II to surviving groups of hunter-fishers who preserved the Mesolithic economy mentioned on pp. 82-3.

The Neolithic farmers who buried their dead in Megalithic tombs and are therefore termed Megalith-builders practised a rural economy based on slash-and-burn shifting cultivation[2]—and the breeding of cattle, pigs, and a few

---

[1] Brondsted, *Danmarks Oldtid* (Copenhagen; 1938-39).
[2] Iversen, "Landnam i Danmarks Stenalder," *Danmarks Geol. Undersogelse*, II R., No. 66.

sheep or goats, very similar to the English. But they possibly kept horses to draw sleds and certainly possessed boats suitable for navigation on the Sound and the Belts, if not for crossing the North Sea and the Baltic. Presumably by trade, in exchange for amber they obtained a few metal weapons and tools both from Central Europe and the British Isles, and these they copied very cleverly in stone. But numerous weapons show that these farmers were extremely warlike.

Their settlements were small and not occupied for many years—at Barkaer in Jutland[1] there were 54 houses in Period I : their family vaults were used for longer periods. In Period III such tombs may contain up to ninety-eight corpses. They, of course, afford no evidence of rank. Nor were female figurines or phalli modelled in any durable material to provide evidence on sex relations.

Contrasted with the Megalith-builders were more pastoral tribes who occupied first the sandy soils of Jutland and parts of southern Sweden and can only be recognized on the Danish islands in Period III. These "pastoralists," of course, also hunted and cultivated cereals; indeed, they may have used a plough, since plough-furrows have been detected under, and were therefore earlier than, a barrow of Period IV.[2] At the same time they were even more warlike than the Megalith-builders; a stone battle-axe accompanied every male interment.

The pastoral groups are known exclusively from burials —in individual graves under barrows. These afford no indication of chieftainship, but burials of man and woman in the same grave do occur, albeit quite exceptionally.[3]

Before the end of Period III itinerant metal-workers were fashioning in Denmark and even in southern Sweden

---

[1] Glob, in *Fra Nationalmuseets Arbejdsmark* (Copenhagen; 1949).
[2] Hatt, " Pyovfurer Jylland," *Aarbøger* (1941); cf. *Antiquity* (1946).
[3] Glob, in *Aarbøger* (1944).

versions of Danubian and British weapons and ornaments adapted to local tastes, but these were too rare to deposit in graves. By Period IV trade was sufficiently well organized to secure adequate supplies of bronze to enable native craftsmen to produce handsome weapons and ornaments. As in Britain, the rural economy of the ensuing Bronze Age appears predominantly pastoral, and the pastoralists' practice of individual burial completely supplanted the use of Megalithic family vaults.

The graves of the " Earlier Bronze Age " (Periods IV-V) are covered with large and carefully constructed barrows and furnished with a surprising wealth of arms and ornaments of bronze, occasional objects of precious metal, beads of glass imported from the Mediterranean, and even folding stools—a stool is often a sign of rank. Elsewhere such would be classed as " royal tombs," but there are two thousand four hundred such graves in Denmark, so they can belong at best to a ruling class of great landowners or ranchers. On the other hand, burials of a " lower class " have never been identified.

In the Late Bronze Age the rich barrows of Denmark and south-western Sweden entirely disappear to make room for monotonously poor cremation graves in urn-fields—sometimes inserted in older barrows. Instead, in rather peripheral regions—near Uppsala, at Kivik on the Baltic coast of Skania, and at Seddin in North Germany —we find three enormous barrows[1] covering genuine royal tombs with extravagantly rich furniture and human sacrifices. Had a social revolution wiped out the old squirearchy only to establish despotic monarchy? On the other hand, bronze was far more plentiful than before and, without entirely replacing stone even for axes, was freely used for industrial purposes and rough work like felling trees. Wheeled vehicles came into use. War chariots are

[1] Kivik, Kung Bjorns, Hög, and Seddin; see *Real.,* s.v.

represented on the slabs of the Kivik tomb and on rock engravings. The latter depict also ploughing scenes and boats, including galleys, manned by warriors bearing round bronze shields. Trade brought bronze vessels manufactured in Central Europe or even in Italy, glass beads from the Mediterranean, and gold from Transylvania and Eire. But much wealth—notably gold vessels—was deposited in bogs as votive offerings to ghosts or spirits.

Finally, in the Iron Age graves are poorer than ever; no royal tombs are known; even votive hoards are rare and poor. Yet excavation discloses commodious farms with stalls for the beasts and granaries. Systems of fields, still visible, show that plough agriculture was now regularly practised and that a proper system of fallowing had superseded the old shifting cultivation. Moreover, in addition to the light plough or ard, a heavy plough, probably wheeled and capable of turning over the sod, was employed—a device suitable to the cold, damp climate then ruling in the north, but not to the Mediterranean and subtropical zones, where ploughing, as well as corn-growing, presumably started. Yet it needed still nearly a thousand years before anything like city life blossomed in northern Europe.

CHAPTER VIII

Cultural Stages in Temperate Europe

The observed cultural sequences just summarized in a very abstract form for three provinces of the temperate zone could, by still further abstraction, be condensed into one evolutionary series.

(1) As the first basis of classification we must take the food supply—in other words, the rural economy. Throughout barbarism this was based on the cultivation of cereals and the breeding of cattle, pigs, and sheep for food. But within this we can provisionally distinguish three or four stages.

In a somewhat hypothetical Stage O, represented, if at all, only on the Central European löss lands in Danubian I, the main source of food would be wheat and barley grown in small plots tilled with hoes and abandoned as soon as exhausted, supplemented by the produce of stock-breeding but not of the chase.

In Stage I, represented by Danubian II, the British "Neolithic," and all Northern Megalithic, cattle and pigs were at least as important as cereals, but the two forms of husbandry were not effectively integrated, so that cultivation depended on slash-and-burn, and wild food resources were not fully exploited by hunting.

In Stage II game was more adequately hunted and animal husbandry became more important than cultivation. Some societies in each province can be described as pastoralists, though even these always cultivated cereals, perhaps sometimes with a plough but still without a regular system of fallowing, so that cultivation remained shifting. In Britain and Denmark such pastoral societies dominate the archæological record of the Bronze Age, but in Central Europe they coexist with more agricultural groups. On the other hand, while such pastoralists appear only later than farmers of Stage I in Central Europe and Britain, in Northern Europe they are suspected side by side with the Megalithic farmers from the start and are clearly distinguished in Period II.

Stage III is then defined by plough cultivation and the use of dung from byres and the droppings of grazing sheep to restore fertility to exhausted fields. Corn-growing and stock-raising were thus integrated to allow of a system of fallowing and also the multiplication of flocks. While this system had appeared first in the Late Bronze Age and was established throughout most of the temperate zone at the beginning of Iron Age I, on the poorer soils covered with coniferous forest slash-and-burn still persisted and pigs continued to outnumber sheep.

(2) A second basis of classification is the technological, and is most conveniently defined by specialization of labour. The essence of any " Stone Age " economy is that all essential tools can be made from local materials and within the household without further division of labour. But within the Neolithic Age intercommunal specialization, represented archæologically by flint-mines and axe-factories (not necessarily worked by full-time specialists), may be treated as a sub-stage A. Such specialist communities are recognizable in Britain and throughout Western Europe from the start, so that Stage I there can always be distinguished as IA. In Central and Northern Europe Stage IA is inferential, but IIA is well attested.

A Bronze Age is impossible without full-time specialists and therefore initiates a new technological stage, B. The earlier Bronze Age may therefore everywhere be designated IIB. But at this time the specialist metal-workers seem to have been at least mainly itinerants, not permanently resident in any settlement and so probably not incorporated into the local social organization.

A real "separation of handicraft from agriculture" begins timidly in the Late Bronze Age, when we find the first evidences for resident smiths. But in most areas the Late Bronze Age also witnesses the effective use of plough-cultivation, so that it may be labelled Stage IIIC, if C denote the new technological stage. It coincides with the multiplication of metal tools, such that they became available to cultivators and miners, and probably the specialization of some other crafts, at least those of carpenters and wainwrights.

The use of iron for tools and weapons was of such importance that the First Iron Age must be distinguished as Stage IIID. But though it enabled farmers to clear fresh fields and so increase the food-supply it did not at once bring about a further division of labour.

That happens first in Iron Age II (La Tène), which must therefore be designated Stage IIIE. Then we meet for the first time a number of new full-time specialists—glass-workers, potters—and a subdivision of older crafts. At the same time many new tools and labour-saving devices—hinged tongs, shears, scythes, rotary querns—appear first in the archæological record.

(3) Means of transport should be correlated with the rural and technical stages, but the record is too deficient for them to be made an independent basis of classification. Water transport can be inferred at all stages. Horses were kept, and presumably used as pack-animals or for drawing sledges by Stage II in North and Central Europe, but probably not in Britain till Stage III. In that stage—i.e., in Stage IIIC—wheeled vehicles are to be assumed everywhere.

(4) The volume and extent of trade should be added to complete the characterization of an economy, but data for

any precise estimation of those magnitudes are still want-ing. Very intermittent long-distance "trade" in small luxury articles like sea-shells is detectable already in Stage I, and in the same stage choice materials for axes or querns might be "traded" for distances of 100 miles or so. With the rise of intercommunal specialization this local trade must have become rather more regular and included manufactures or semi-manufactures. More regu-lar trade was a *sine qua non* for any "Bronze Age," and therefore characteristic of Stage IIB. Commerce then was not confined to "industrial metals" but distributed also portable luxury articles like amber, jet, gold. Standardized forms of ingot (neck-rings, double-axes) with limited dis-tributions are recognizable, but not standardized weights and certainly no generalized standard of value—money. The amber trade demonstrably not only linked up the producing regions of Jutland and Samland with metalli-ferous regions in Britain and Central Europe, but it also connected all with Minoan Crete and Mycenæan Greece—i.e., with the nearest urbanized centres disposing of a con-centrated social surplus. In the long run, therefore, the imported metals and luxuries consumed in Stage IIB were not wholly paid for out of the social surplus locally pro-duced but partly at least by that accumulated in the East Mediterranean. In fact an "Early Bronze Age"—i.e., Stage IIB—existed only in countries producing materials demanded in the East Mediterranean and along the routes leading thither; it is missing in northern France, Nor-way, and the forest zone of Eastern Europe.

On the contrary, in the Late Bronze Age, Stage IIIC, metal products were much more widely distributed and reached even regions that had not hitherto advanced be-yond the "Neolithic" level of Stage IIA. That implies a real internal market—in other words, a local social surplus which would be a corollary of the higher yield from primary production. Nevertheless trade with the Mediterranean markets still brought the barbarian economy support from the accumulated surplus of the urban civilizations. Thence came the standards of weight now adopted by barbarian societies. Money appears in the form of gold rings accepted in various localities as a medium of exchange.

With the introduction of iron in Stage IIID a relative shrinkage of trade and a reversion towards self-sufficency are noticable in several regions, notably England and northern Europe. On the other hand, the rise of urban markets in Italy, South France (Massilia), and round the Black Sea coasts produced an effective demand, nearer at hand than ever before, for raw materials produced in the temperate zone. Thus an increasing stream of urban manufactures, still mainly luxury articles, crossed the Alpine passes or reached the Pontic steppes and Transylvania. In their wake came a conventional form of money—spits.

The transition from Stage IIID to IIIE round the Alps is a direct consequence of this trade. Its continued expansion and that of internal commerce led to the adoption of coined money.

(5) Warfare is attested already in Stage I—not in Stage O—but does not become a regular and prominent social activity of all societies in temperate Europe until Stage IIA. Subsequently, indications of warfare become increasingly prominent, save that the Early Iron Age farmers in Stage IIID, relapsing towards self-sufficiency (p. §§§), restricted their commercial relations with others and do not appear to have initiated hostile relations. It is to be noted that bronze was first employed, in Stage IIB, mainly for weapons which must have been rare and costly. These decisive new weapons in Stage IIB, and likewise the war-chariots of Stages IIIC and IIIE, can normally have been

available only to a minority, who concentrated a still small social surplus.

(6) The total population supported by each of the foregoing economies in any province cannot be estimated from available data. But number and size of cemeteries increasing regularly from stage to stage do demonstrate a progressive expansion of population, and thus justify the contention that each stage represented an advance on its precursor. Estimates of the numbers that lived together in a single local group can, however, be based only on settlements or cemeteries systematically excavated so as to expose either the total number of houses or graves or at least to allow this total to be inferred from the proportion of the area excavated. Neither method is available in the case of most of the " pastoral societies " in Stages IIA and IIB, since no villages of such are known and their members were generally buried under barrows that need not cover all deceased members of the local group and in any case are less likely to survive as complete clusters than are flat graves grouped in a cemetery.

In Stage I Neolithic farmers in Central Europe seem to have lived in villages comprising twelve to thirty households. In Stage IIA the figures are of the order of forty-five (Homolka in Bohemia) to fifty (in the Altheim settlement on the Goldberg, Wurt.). Comparable evidence for Stage IIB is lacking, and in Stage IIIC we have, at the same site, villages of thirty-eight small and then of nine large houses. Villages of the same small size, a dozen houses, are known also in IIID, but these are juxtaposed to much larger fortified enclosures covering twelve or more acres that undoubtedly comprised many more houses, though no figures are available. In Stage IIIE isolated farms may also be assumed. The maximal observed (and inferred in brackets) numbers of graves in cemeteries, presumably belonging to a single settlement, are :

Stage I 65-78

    II A 50

    II B 141

    III C 240 (320)

    III D 1100

    III E

These figures are not strictly comparable, as there is no evidence to enable one to deduce the number of years during which any cemetery was used. The increase in the number of graves may therefore indicate a greater permanence in the settlements rather than a larger number of settlers living together.

(7) Some, but not all, houses in Danubian villages of Stage I are so large as to accommodate a small clan rather than a single natural family. Similarly, the larger collective tombs of the same stage in Britain and North Europe may have been clan, rather than family, vaults. For the rest, apart from the cluster at Skara Brae, the exiguous architectural and funerary evidence from Stage IIA on is compatible with the assumption of the natural family as an institution or economic unit.

(8) Female figurines occur in both Central Europe and Britain in Stage I only and have been interpreted as Mother Goddesses and therefore as indications of descent through the female, but in Western Europe they occur already side by side with phalli in Stage I, and similar male symbols replace them in Stage IIA in Central Europe.

Double graves of a man and woman buried together occur in all stages and provinces, as already in the preceding stage of savagery. As in the earlier stage, it has occasionally been expressly noted that the woman was much younger than her companion (e.g., in a " royal tomb " of Stage IIB and in several " chieftain's " graves of Stage IIIE). In Stages IIIC, IIID, and IIIE double interments are most commonly those of chieftains. They are notably rare in the graves of the very warlike pastoralists of Stage IIA in Denmark.

(9) Ownership by individuals, or at least by natural families, of means of production in the form of cattle might be inferred for Stage I from cattle-byres allegedly attached to small houses in Denmark; but this evidence is still disputed. It is attested by undeniable cattle-stalls already in Stage IIB(A) in Shetland, and then regularly in Stage IIIC. Hatt has deduced individual ownership of fields for Stage IIID in Denmark, but his arguments are not altogether convincing.

(10) Chieftains, suspected in IIA, can first be recognized with certainty in Stage IIB and then only in the Saale valley, where graves of exceptional construction and richness attest their occupants' rank. Neither burials nor the complete excavation of several settlement sites have produced satisfactory evidence for differences of rank in Stages I and IIA. Later, in Stage IIB, the rich graves of Wessex and of Denmark may belong to an aristocracy of numerous petty chieftains, but this is disputed. In Stage IIIC the existence of chiefs in Central Europe is well established, and in Stage IIID high chiefs or kings can be distinguished from local chiefs or headmen. But in Britain the first reliable chieftains' graves belong to Stage IIIE.

(11) Slavery may be recognized in Central Europe as early as Stage I if double graves in which one corpse was unaccompanied by gear, the other richly furnished, be accepted as evidence of that institution. But save in connection with chieftains' burials such indications are at all times rare and ambiguous. For example, in two Scottish graves both the deceased belonged to the same physical type—that of the Beaker-folk, who had apparently invaded Britain at the end of Stage I.

But evidence for slavery is notoriously hard to find in

the archæological record, and proof of its non-existence is quite unobtainable. It is still useful to inquire how the labour for "public works" was recruited. Presumably work on the fortification of a settlement was, like military service, the obligation and duty of every able-bodied member of the community. The same principles would apply to the construction of streets, such as we have in Neolithic villages at Skara Brae and on the marshes round the Alps. Megalithic tombs, if really communal sepulchres, could be explained in the same way, and so also could even the most enormous " Bronze Age " sanctuaries like Avebury and Stonehenge. Purely voluntary communal labour can likewise be invoked to explain the really gigantic fortifications of the Iron Age. But the construction of the chieftain's castle or citadel within the enceinte, such as we have at the Goldberg in Stage IIID, and of royal tombs, might seem to involve something more—an obligation on his followers to provide labour services for their chief. Though the latter be still regarded as the representative of the collectivity, there would lie herein, even in barbarism, at least the germs of a class division other than that between slave and freeman.

On the other hand, it is possible, but perhaps less probable, that this sort of labour was provided by slaves—i.e., captives taken in war. Zschocke and Preuschen[1] had indeed argued that the heavy labour of mining in Stage IIIC and later was performed by such slaves. But no positive evidence has been adduced and Pittioni has suggested alternative sources of labour.

The attentive reader will doubtless have noticed that the process described in para. 1 reveals, not stages in the evolution of rural economy, but rather stages in the adaptation of a rural economy, based on exotic cereals and exotic

---

[1] *Das urzeitliche Bergbaugebiet von Mühlbach-Bischofshofen* (*Materialien zur Urgeschichte Österreichs*, VI), Vienna; 1932.

sheep, to the environment of the deciduous forest zone. In the same way the technologies considered in para. 2 did not evolve in temperate Europe, but were borrowed and adapted from the East Mediterranean. So too the regular commerce distributing the materials on which the technology of the Bronze Age, Stage B, was based was apparently initiated by emissaries from civilized markets. The technical advances—rotary quern, compass, coinage—that distinguish Stage IIIE were as demonstrably diffused from Greek and Etruscan cities by that trade as the actual materials (coral and wine) and manufactures (metal vases and pottery) that it brought to the temperate zone. A similar mechanism may be assumed as operative in earlier periods.

On the other hand, the rural economy of Stage II, although at first sight more " savage," was really more productive than that of I and supplanted it for that reason. It is indeed believed by many that some of the more pastoral tribes that appear in Stage IIA were fresh immigrants in Central and Northern Europe, as the systadial Beaker-folk in Britain almost certainly were. Even so, the dominance of " pastoralists " throughout Stage IIB merely proves the superiority of their economy for the specific regions (Great Britain, Northern Europe, and the sandy and limestone plateaux and coniferous tracts of Central Europe) that they did dominate. Again, the advance in rural economy represented by the general adoption of plough-agriculture went hand in hand with its technical presupposition, the availability to farmers of metal tools for fine woodwork. But *pari passu* with the consequent enlargement of the yield from primary production did the local market's capacity to absorb metal ware expand.

It is quite possible that the recognizable social institutions which we can find emerging in several stages or periods were likewise borrowed or copied from more advanced societies Even so, it is clear that they became established only in so far as the economy of the temperate zone was in a position to support them. The rich " chieftains' graves " of the Saale valley in Stage IIB look like poor versions of the royal tombs of Abydos, Ur, or Anyang, so that Early Bronze Age chieftains may be attenuated ghosts of the Divine Kings of Egypt, Mesopotamia, and China. But since such tombs remain quite isolated in the temperate zone at that stage, it may be inferred that the locally producible social surplus was still too small to support such an institution; the wealth buried in the Saale tombs can be regarded as a fraction of the accumulated surplus of the Orient annexed in return for raw materials. It is first in Stage IIID that royal graves are sufficiently numerous to attest the recognition of kingship as a normal institution, but even so only in Central Europe. By that time not only could a much larger social surplus be produced, but new means of communication and domination were available in the form of wheeled vehicles and cavalry.

We may thus hope to detect, in the zone of deciduous forest, some correlations between social-political institutions and technico-economic stages. But the latter themselves are not universal, but strictly conditioned by soil and climate and by historical circumstances. If we are to make abstraction of the physical and human environment in order to discover universal " laws," we must examine other natural provinces and different historical circumstances. Culture sequences are to-day available in the Mediterranean zone of winter rains and in the subtropical zone of steppe and alluvial river valley to the south and south-east, so let us turn thither.

CHAPTER IX

Culture Sequences in Barbarism: (2) *The Mediterranean
Zone*

The only tolerably complete sequences yet available in the
Mediterranean zone apply to its eastern end—the western
coasts and islands of the Ægean Sea. Like the rest of the
zone, this is an area where the rainfall is confined to the
winter months, while the summers are hot and dry. Permanent water supplies are therefore restricted to perennial
springs and a limited number of short snow-fed rivers.
Greece and Crete are rocky and mountainous, but the cal-
careous and volcanic soils, though stony, are propitious for
olives, fig-trees, and vines as well as for cereals. While
mountain ranges impede inland transport, the sea, generally calm in summer, opens to the indented coasts enticing
waterways and provides supplies of sea-food. In the past
there were plenty of forests to provide timber for boat-
building, though they were not so dense and continuous as
in the temperate zone north of the Alps and Balkans.
Finally, the sea gave access to the coasts of North Africa
and Hither Asia, where by 3000 B.C. the oldest urban
civilizations had already accumulated a quite substantial
social surplus. Most of the period of Barbarism in the
Ægean is, in fact, contemporary with civilization in Egypt
and Mesopotamia.

In Crete, Peninsular Greece, and Macedonia alike five
main cultural periods may be distinguished and designated
respectively " Neolithic," Early, Middle, Late Ægean, and
Iron Age. But though more or less contemporary, the cultures during each period in the three regions are quite

distinct. The first period can be subdivided into Neolithic A and B on the Mainland, a subdivision not yet applicable to the island of Crete, and clearest in Thessaly and Macedonia, where Neolithic B is mainly contemporary with Early Ægean in the Peninsula. In Crete, civilization was achieved precariously in Middle Minoan (Middle Ægean) times, but elsewhere its arrival was delayed till the Iron Age, and even in Crete a Dark Age of illiteracy separated the local Bronze Age civilization from that of the Classical Iron Age. The same Dark Age intervenes on the Mainland too, but nowhere did it entail the loss of the fundamental techniques and means of transport developed in the Bronze Age, or a complete interruption of commerce.

It will be convenient to treat the five periods as if they were stages and to follow the arrangement adopted in the preceding chapter. The sequence in Peninsular Greece[1] will be described first; then, in a more summary manner, those observed in Crete and Macedonia.

(a) *Peninsular Greece*

(1) The rural economy from the beginning of the record is based on mixed farming with a system of cultivation that allows of the continuous occupation of the same site. Though the existence of the plough is not attested, the earliest Neolithic farmers in Greece have apparently reached the stage termed III in the less congenial environment of the deciduous forests. Indeed, the practice of orchard husbandry is not improbable. At the same time natural resources in wild food were fully exploited by hunting and presumably also by fishing.

By the Early Ægean (called on the Mainland Helladic) period the cultivation of vines and fig-trees and probably also of olives is attested, and ploughs were certainly used.

---

[1] General summary, Childe, *Dawn.*

There is no sign of a separation of pastoral from agricultural tribes, though resort must have been had to transhumance—the transfer of flocks and herds from the lowlands to summer pastures. At least by the Late Helladic, specialized agriculture for the production of crops for the market must have begun in addition to subsistence agriculture, but all communities probably relied on homegrown corn for subsistence till the sixth century.

(2) Neolithic equipment was presumably home-made without specialization. But most Early Helladic communities probably supported a resident bronze-smith, who made craftsmen's tools and, in Late Helladic, also agricultural implements such as sickles. The number of specialists somewhat rapidly multiplied. Professional potters began to work in Peninsular Greece during the Middle Helladic period and must have been joined in Late Helladic times by equally specialized masons, carpenters, wainwrights, jewellers, lapidaries, and several others. The luxury crafts must have suffered a severe setback in the dark beginnings of the Iron Age and some may have died out. But though styles changed and art declined, most techniques, and therefore the families or guilds that transmitted them, survived.

(3) Sea-going ships[1] propelled by oars are attested from the Early Helladic, sailing-ships from the beginning of Late Helladic. By that time horses and wheeled vehicles were available for use in land transport, and some attempts were made at constructing roads and bridging torrents. Equitation is attested by the end of the Bronze Age.

(4) Even in Neolithic A obsidian, brought by sea from Melos (or perhaps by land from Hungary), was used in Thessaly occasionally, while even pots might be exchanged —of course with their contents—between adjacent regions.

---

[1] Bronze Age ships, Marinatos, *Bull. Correspondence, Hellénique,* LVII, (1933), pp. 170 ff. Iron Age, Cohen, *A.J.A.,* XLII, p. 194.

Regular trade,[1] mainly sea-borne, must be assumed for the Early Helladic period. It brought, besides the raw materials for any Bronze Age technology (tin may have been available in Greece itself, but copper must have come from Naxos, Crete, or most probably Cyprus), manufactured articles and sealed bales of merchandize from Crete, and took Helladic manufactures to Troy on the Dardanelles. Directly or indirectly, indeed, Early Helladic commerce reached Asia Minor and Egypt on the one hand, and Sicily and perhaps Sardinia and Spain on the other.

During the Middle Helladic period manufactures were less frequently imported from overseas or exported thither, though the supply of metals was not interrupted. But in Late Helladic commerce expanded enormously. Helladic vases, presumably filled with wine or olive oil, reached Sicily, Egypt, the Levant, Anatolia, and Macedonia. In return, Egyptian, Syrian, and Hittite manufactures found their way to Greece; also amber beads from the Baltic, and very probably Irish gold, and copper and tin from temperate Europe. It should, however, here be recalled that, judging by the literary references, trading and raiding could be combined in the Ægean. In archæology a piece of loot is indistinguishable from an import obtained by legitimate commerce.

In the Iron Age trade[2] did decline temporarily, and many communities relapsed towards self-sufficiency, though never so far as in southern England during Stage IIID (p. 103). Nevertheless, the flow of amber to Greece never entirely ceased, and as early as the tenth century Thessalian pottery was transported to Palestine. By the seventh century pots and other mass-produced articles were being exported on an unprecedented scale to a Mediter-

[1] Wace and Blegen, "Pottery as Evidence for Trade," *Klio*, XXXII (1939).
[2] On sea-trade see Heichelheim, *Wirtschaftsgeschichte des Altertums*, p. 248.

ranean market. At the beginning of the period such trade as there was may have been carried in alien (Phœnician) bottoms, but in the sequel these were ousted first by big landowners, who combined raiding and trading, and then by professional merchants, who used converted fishing-boats and eventually built special cargo ships, which, from about 650 B.C., are contrasted with vessels built primarily for war and piracy.

Standardized weights and measures were recognized already in the Early Ægean period. In the Late Ægean the ox was the accepted standard of value and had been equated with a weighed quantity of gold (the talent), but commodities—cauldrons, tripods, or axes of bronze—served as media of exchange.[1] These two functions of money were combined during the Iron Age in conventional spits (Gr.—*obeliskoi*), which were replaced soon after 700 B.C. by coins of precious metal,[2] for large transactions.

(5) There is no evidence for war in Neolithic A, but some settlements of Neolithic B are fortified as were some contemporary Early Helladic towns on the coasts. Middle Helladic graves and settlements look definitely warlike, while by Late Helladic warfare was doubtless endemic. At that time costly bronze rapiers and still more costly chariots were decisive weapons. Iron reduced the cost of weapons of offence, and chariotry gradually gave place to cavalry and then to infantry. Iron Age ships[3] as represented on early vases were evidently designed primarily for use as pirate vessels or men-of-war.

(6) The normal settlement in Neolithic Greece was a cluster of small houses, repeatedly rebuilt on the same site, whose ruins form oval mounds, normally about 120 feet long by 100 feet wide but rising at times to 220 feet by

[1] Seltman, *Greek Coins*.
[2] Ægina, 650 B.C., Corinth, 620; Heichelheim, *op. cit.*, p. 220.
[3] Cohen, *A.J.A.*, XLII, p. 194.

115 feet. In the hinterland of the Gulf of Volo no fewer than fifty such settlements existed on the small plain between Larissa and the Gulf.[1] Helladic settlements were not much larger in area, at least in the interior; at Malthi, in Messenia, for instance, the enceinte wall encircles a space 138 feet long by 82 feet wide.[2]

In any case these small areas were often closely built over with small composite houses separated only by narrow lanes. In the Late Helladic period we find in addition fortified citadels or acropoles, covering from five to eleven acres, with dependent open villages outside their walls. The citadel itself is largely taken up by a palace with its appurtenances. Neither the compact Early Helladic settlements nor the Late Helladic citadels can rank as cities even in point of physical size. A Classical Greek city might cover from one hundred acres (Priene) to two hundred and twenty (Olynthus) or more acres.[3] But when the critical point was reached is still uncertain. No sites of the earliest Iron Age have been fully excavated. On the other hand, the earlier *poleis*[4] were doubtless inhabited mainly by working farmers, though always, as in the Bronze Age, mixed with artisans and others. The proportion of the industrial and commercial element to the agricultural provides a less workable criterion of civilization than that we have adopted namely, writing. On the latest evidence writing was used in Attica by about 750 B.C.[5]

(7) Neolithic settlements—burials are unknown—afford no evidence as to the form of the family unit. By Early Helladic collective burial in communal ossuaries was the

---

[1] *Athenische Mitteilungen*, LXII (1937), p. 58.

[2] Valmin, *The Swedish Messenia Expedition* (Lund; 1938).

[3] Haverfield, *Ancient Town Planning*; Robinson, *Excavations at Olynthus*, VIII, The Greek House.

[4] Heichelheim, *op. cit.*, p. 241, would deny the title " city " to any Greek polis before 650 B.C.

[5] Blegen, *A.J.A.*, XXXVIII, pp. 10-28.

rule. But, as a regular cemetery of twenty or more such tombs might be attached to a single modest settlement, each vault probably held the remains of successive generations of a single natural family. This was demonstrably the case in Late Helladic times, when rock-cut tombs were simply "family vaults" such as exist to-day. But the absence of gross physical expressions of the unity of the clan does not disprove the vitality of the system, which is in fact attested even in early Classical times as well as in the heroic Bronze Age we call Mycenæan or Late Helladic. In the latter period, as already remarked, the grouping of family vaults into several small cemeteries round the Mycenæan citadels has suggested that each cluster of tombs corresponds to a clan rather than a local group.

(8) Female figurines were even more popular in Neolithic Greece than in Danubian I, but here their manufacture continued throughout the Ægean Bronze Age and also the Iron Age. And in the latter period they do demonstrably represent goddesses. But phallic symbols also appear in the Ægean Bronze Age, and in Homer and later literature goddesses notoriously coexisted with, and were subordinate to, gods.

Double graves of a man and woman interred together occur already in Middle Helladic times[1]—previously there can be no evidence—and in Late Helladic royal tombs (private tombs of this period, being family vaults, cannot be invoked).

(9) Seals were used already—albeit rarely—in Neolithic A, presumably to mark commodities as personal possessions of their owner. This use is better attested in the Early Helladic period and later. By that time, too, active trade implies a conception of commodities as personally owned, alienable, and capable of yielding profit. But for means of production—livestock, land, ships, and so on—

[1] E.g., Frödin and Persson, *Asine* (1938), p. 122.

there is less evidence. As soon as the ox became a standard of value for commercial exchanges, private ownership of livestock may be assumed. That had happened by Late Helladic times and was not likely to have been a novel idea then, when the ox was equated to quantities of gold or copper. On land tenure archæology has nothing to say. In Homeric or Late Helladic times ownership of the land was perhaps vested in the king or prince, but only as representative of the community. Then, perhaps with the decay of kingship in the Iron Age, land returned, not to communal, but to individual, ownership. But even in Homer the king had personal demesnes, and it was on such, if anywhere, that production for the market could begin.

The same ambiguities apply to shipping. Large seagoing boats that could be used for war, piracy, and trade apparently belonged to the king in Late Helladic times. But it is clear, from the Homeric narrative as well as from ethnographic parallels, that a place therein was a right rather than duty of his "companions" who formed the "crew." In the early part of the Iron Age pirate galleys that were also merchantmen were apparently owned by large landowners,[1] but smaller men might own fishing-smacks, and such might be used also for overseas trade. But who owned the quite large ships of the Early Helladic period manned by eight or twelve rowers?

(10) Two fortified villages of Neolithic B near the Gulf of Volo in Thessaly contain within their walls what looks like a chieftain's palace. But apart from these eccentric and anomalous sites there is no evidence for the concentration of wealth in the hands of princes nor of divinities till the Late Helladic period. Then, as we saw in Chapter IV, stately tholos tombs and palaces attest the rule of "divine kings" over a number of tiny principalities. In the Iron

[1] See p. 123.

Age this divine kingship withered away. The old Bronze Age palaces were replaced by temples, but there is no indication that their divine occupants added to their wealth by engaging in commerce or piracy, as their mortal precursors had done, or even replaced by tithes the taxes on the land which they continued to "own" in a purely theological sense. The old royal tombs sometimes became shrines for hero cults, but no others were built. On the contrary, in the Geometric cemeteries there are certain graves differing from the rest in the richness of their furnishings but not in structure or ritual. These are the tombs of the new ruling class—an aristocracy of big landowners, far more numerous than the Bronze Age kings—who yet concentrated the enlarged social surplus producible with an Iron Age equipment. They are disclosed to us in the poems of Hesiod and in the immediately succeeding literary sources. It was not, however, their accumulated wealth so much as that of a new class of merchants that transformed the barbarism of the Geometric Age into Classical Greek civilization.

(11) Slavery is not illustrated by any archæological documents before Classical times. The Homeric poems, however, prove that slaves were kept in Late Helladic times, although ships, for instance, were rowed by free companions of the captain. Again, in the Iron Age even a small farmer keeps a slave in Hesiod.

But we are still entitled to ask who built the fortifications round Early Helladic townships and the much more massive walls of the Mycenæan citadels. The fortification of a settlement may, as we have seen, be regarded as a communal work in which all members of the community were expected and entitled to participate as they would in actual military operations of defence. That is not so obviously the case with the Cyclopean walls round citadels that contained little but a prince's palace, and still less of the palaces themselves or the royal tombs connected with them. It is unlikely that the substantial labour force engaged on these imposing works was composed entirely of slaves and captives, or was recruited from a " proletariat " —specialist labourers supported exclusively from the social surplus concentrated by the prince. It is just as likely to have been recruited by the corvée from small peasants who owed customary services to the lord of the land. If so, it means already a form of class division and exploitation, even though the ruler who exploits is still accepted as representative of the community, and the workers therefore do not feel exploited.

(b) *Macedonia*

The coastal plain and valleys of western Macedonia[1] offer wider continuous tracts of arable land, but are colder, more continental, and less propitiously situated for trade than the coasts and plains of peninsular Greece. The culture sequence therefore offers an instructive, but by no means surprising, contrast to that just recapitulated. But it must be admitted in advance that this contrast may be grossly exaggerated by the inadequacy of the data. For no Macedonian settlement has been so fully excavated as those of peninsular Greece—the ceramic sequence has been established rather by narrow trenches and pits dug into the settlement mounds—and no cemeteries are known till the Iron Age.

The Neolithic period in Macedonia seems in all respects parallel to that of the peninsula, save that the cultivation of fig-trees is explicitly attested in its second, B, phase. But in the Ægean Bronze Age divergences appear. If the rural economy were much the same, there is much less evidence for specialization of labour or for trade. Axes

[1] Heurtley, *Prehistoric Macedonia* (Cambridge; 1939).

and other implements of stone were not replaced by metal ones, so we can assume neither resident smiths nor professional potters till the Iron Age. But weapons of war occur already in the Early Macedonian phase, and one coastal settlement was fortified in Middle Macedonian times. At the same time male symbols occur without ousting female figurines. Still, throughout the Bronze Age Macedonian settlements remained almost self-sufficing rustic villages, no larger than the Neolithic and economically scarcely distinguishable therefrom. First in the Iron Age does the establishment of professional potters in some centres indicate a substantial expansion of population, due no doubt to the use for tools of iron, which could be obtained without much sacrifice of self-sufficiency. At that time, too, there are some hints of a separation of pastoral from agricultural groups, inasmuch as some communities, without entirely abandoning cultivation, specialized in breedings goats.

(c) *Crete*

Crete,[1] as an island lying south, enjoys a warmer and milder climate than Mainland Greece. Its soil, though much more restricted, is just as fertile and once supported forests to supply timber for boat-building. It lies still nearer than the Peninsula to the ancient centres of civilization, and at the appropriate season the winds and currents assist voyages on the one hand to Egypt, on the other to Anatolia, Cyprus, and the Levant.

The Cretan Neolithic culture differs, as far as we know, in no relevant aspect from that of Mainland Greece, but that of the Bronze Age, termed Minoan and divided into Early, Middle, and Late, developed more rapidly.

(1) The rural economy was not fundamentally different,

[1] Pendlebury, *The Archæology of Crete* (London; 1939).

I

but specialized in agriculture, producing olive oil and perhaps also wine, and other products for export may be assumed as early as Middle Minoan II.

(2) Similarly, handicraft separated from agriculture soon. In Early Minoan, metal was perhaps not much commoner than on the Mainland, but by Middle Minoan it was used for the manufacture of heavy sledge-hammers and probably for making cauldrons and similar vessels; and, by Late Minoan at least, also for sickles. Professional carpenters, jewellers, lapidaries, and other specialists are, in addition to smiths, attested either by their products or by seals engraved with the emblems of their craft. During the Middle Minoan period professional potters began producing vases *en masse* with the aid of the wheel, and were joined by other full-time specialists, including even clerks.

(3) For transport by water, ships[1] propelled by oars were available in Early Minoan. Middle Minoan ships attained a length of 70 feet and sometimes used sails to assist the rowers. Decked ships, 100 feet long, are depicted in Late Minoan scenes. Wheeled vehicles were in use from the beginning of Middle Minoan, but horses cannot be traced before the Late Minoan Age. Before then, roads and bridges were being constructed, as well as some sort of harbour works.

(4) Overseas " trade " brought obsidian even to Neolithic Crete. In Early Minoan times it brought, in addition to gold, silver, liparite, marble, and other raw materials, articles manufactured on the Greek islands and Mainland and even in Egypt. Maritime trade was indeed so important that even a tiny barren islet became, thanks to its convenient harbour and good water, the home of a thriving community. Through this trade Crete was enabled to tap the accumulated surplus of Egypt and, more indirectly, of the Mesopotamian cities. In the Middle Minoan

[1] See note 4, p. 47.

period even Babylonian cylinder seals and more Egyptian manufactures were imported to Crete. The island's exports included pottery (found in Egypt, Cyprus, and Syria[1] as well as in Mainland Greece and the islands), textiles (mentioned in texts from Mari on the Euphrates), and doubtless oil, dyestuffs, and wine. Minoan commerce culminated in L.M. II, between 1500 and 1400 B.C., when even Baltic amber and Irish gold reached the island. Thereafter it suffered a sharp setback, since the Mycenæans had secured for the Mainland direct access to the Egyptian market. But even in the Iron Age Crete kept well abreast of the rest of Greece.

(5) Minoan settlements were normally unfortified, and weapons are not nearly so prominent in the archæological record as they are on Mainland Greece in the Middle and Late Helladic periods. Nevertheless, spears and knife-daggers occur in Early Minoan tombs; from the beginning of the next phase " royal weapons " (long bronze rapiers) survive, and a late Minoan fresco represents an organized army comprising apparently a contingent of black mercenaries.

(6) In Early Minoan times people lived in closely built-up settlements like the Early Helladic. None has been completely excavated, and even in the Late Minoan phase the only one that has been excavated covered only 6 acres. But in Early and Middle Minoan times there were also smaller rustic communities and large but isolated farms. Very much larger aggregates must be assumed round the palaces of the Middle and Late Minoan periods, but really reliable indications of their size are lacking. In the Iron Age a refugee settlement on the secluded but rather inhospitable plateau of Lasithi probably accommodated 3,500 persons.

[1] Latest survey, Cantor, " The Ægean and the Orient in the IInd. Millennium, B.C.," *A.J.A.*, LI (1947), pp. 1-102.

(7) Some Early Minoan collective tombs must be regarded as family vaults for the same reason as the Early Helladic sepulchres, but others standing isolated or in groups of only two or three, and containing very large numbers of corpses, would seem rather to be communal ossuaries for members of a larger unit. Such concrete evidence for the solidarity of the clan is missing in later periods.

(8) A female divinity is represented by statuettes and on figured monuments in Neolithic Crete and throughout the Minoan periods into the Iron Age. But models of phalli occur also in Early Minoan tombs, and later the "Mother Goddess" is sometimes depicted with a youthful spouse, while in the Iron Age Crete was reputed to be the birthplace of the high god, Zeus. In the Minoan palaces the "women's" quarter seems better adapted for a single queen than for a harem.

(9) Even in Early Minoan times the use of seals engraved with symbols of the crafts would seem to imply the proprietary rights of the craftsman in the products of his labour, and presumably his tools. Similar rights applied to the contents of sealed jars or parcels. Who owned cattle or land is not directly attested, and, as on Mainland Greece, the ownership of ships is problematical. The representation of ships on seals may well denote that the owners of the seal also owned the ship portrayed; they would then be professional merchants or pirates. But how was the crew recruited?

(10) Neither tombs nor palaces suggest the existence of chiefs in Early Minoan times, but from Middle Minoan the construction of sumptuous palaces in central Crete shows that there power and wealth were being concentrated in the hands of princes or kings. The five largest palaces are situated in central Crete, where they would benefit from the transit trade between Egypt on the south

and the Ægean on the north, Knossos controlling the main route across the island.

Account tablets in the palace archives and spacious magazines attached to all the palaces and containing, among other things, huge jars of wine or oil, show that the rulers used their surplus in export trade. It was at these courts that the most talented craftsmen worked, producing artistic articles like fine pottery, some of which were exported to Egypt and Syria. Writing was apparently confined to the courts and used, judging from the surviving documents, primarily for book-keeping.

Other appurtenances of the palaces would seem more appropriate to temples; and apart from these no temples are known. Hence the princes were also either priests or more probably "divine kings," the earthly representatives of the mother-goddess' consort.

From the first the palace of Knossos was richer and more sumptuous than the other four, but it does not certainly follow that the lords of the latter were always vassals of Knossos. But for at least half a century—from 1450 to 1400 B.C.—"Minos" of Knossos does seem to have been a "king of kings," monarch of the whole island. But the monarchy, which may have been an intrusive one set up by Mycenæan overlords from the mainland, ended in 1400, when the palace of Knossos was sacked, never to be rebuilt on any considerable scale. Political unity was not re-established, and the subsequent social history of Crete, as far as it can be inferred, does not diverge from that of the rest of Greece.

(11) There is no more evidence on slavery from Crete than from Mainland Greece, but on the island the question of the source of the labour supply is more acute. Palace-building implies the use of considerable man-power in quarrying stone, tree-felling, and transporting and erecting materials for the benefit of the prince or king. Apart from

a limited number of specialist masons, carpenters, and painters, it was again most probably supplied by the customary services from families that supported themselves by subsistence agriculture. And if the king had private demesnes devoted to specialized crops, they would be worked in the same manner.

(12) Seals, frescoes, plastic, figured metal-work, and vase-painting illustrate the rise from M.M. II to L.M. II of a naturalistic art that consciously and successfully portrayed plants, marine creatures, animals, and even the human form. This naturalism is contrasted, by its deliberate composition and its success in portrayal of human figures, with the lively naturalism of Palæolithic art and more obviously with the purely geometric styles of barbarism. Native Mycenæan artists—and Cretan artists of the Late Minoan phase after the fall of Knossos—did indeed use vegetable and marine motives in decoration, but always treated them conventionally. The art of the first Iron Age is always, and quite rightly, termed "geometric."

CHAPTER X

Culture Sequences in Barbarism : (3) The Nile Valley

The sub-tropical zone of the East Mediterranean is not only much hotter but also much drier than the northern coasts of that sea. A fringe of steppe that enjoys rather unreliable winter rains, normally just sufficient to water a cereal crop, passes over quickly into a belt of virtually rainless desert. The Nile, though rising in a monsoon belt farther south, flows mainly through this desert. Wilson[1] accordingly can describe the essential part of Egypt " as a green gash of teeming life, cutting across the brown desert wastes." The country is virtually rainless. Only the waters of the Nile provide the conditions for any sort of life—not only for fish and aquatic birds but also for game animals and man's cultivated plants and pasture for his domestic stock. When the archæological record begins in barbarism, the line of demarcation between life and non-life may have been less sharp than it is to-day;[2] at least lower Egypt was bordered with a belt of steppe, and the high desert farther south may have provided scanty pasture for flocks as well as for gazelles and antelopes that certainly grazed thereon. But farming developed only in the valley.

There is a sequence of four prehistoric periods—termed respectively Badarian, Amratian, Gerzean, and Semainian,[3]

[1] Frankfort, Wilson, etc., *The Intellectual Adventure of Ancient Man* (Chicago; 1946), p. 31.

[2] In Badarian times, wadis, now dry, which run across the desert margin of the Nile's flood plain, carried water every year; Mond and Myres, *The Cemeteries of Armant* (1937), pp. 7-8.

[3] Cf. Childe, *New Light on the Most Ancient East* (1935). The divisions were so named by Petrie—cf. his *Prehistoric Egypt* (1920)

—is fairly well established. The Gerzean leads on to the first period of literacy known as Early Dynastic, while the Badarian is preceded by a Tasian period, still rather nebulous in the Nile valley but generally thought[1] to be represented by a settlement at Merimde on the west of the Delta and several sites in the Fayum depression.[2] This opinion has been challenged with some show of reason, and though here the Fayum and Merimde are used as evidence for the culture of the Tasian phase, the reader should remember that the evidence is suspect.

(1) The rural economy was based throughout on mixed farming. Both in the Fayum and at Merimde emmer wheat and barley were grown and cattle, sheep, and pigs were bred. How the crops were watered is uncertain, but natural irrigation seems most likely; seed would be scattered on the wet mud left by the annual inundation of the Nile or—in the Fayum—by winter torrents or overflows from the lake. The same system must be assumed for Badarian and Amratian times; at least in the Early Dynastic the cultivable area was enlarged by canals to distribute the river waters, and very likely this practice goes back to the Gerzean.[3] The same is true of plough-agriculture, attested by Early Dynastic but suspected earlier. After Badarian times the bones of swine disappear from the food refuse, but otherwise the variety of animals kept and crops grown substantially increased. The savage pursuits

---

and *The Making of Egypt* (1939)—but have been criticized. In particular Semainian does not represent a completely distinct culture, since no break separates it from Gerzean comparable to that between Amratian and Gerzean (Cantor, "The Final Phase of Predynastic Culture," *J.N.E.S.*, III (1944), pp. 110-36).

[1] But Baumgärtel, *Cultures of Prehistoric Egypt* (Oxford; 1946), argues that Fayum is Amratian in age and Merimde even later.

[2] Cf. Childe, *op. cit.*, and, for Tasian, Brunton, *Mostagedda and the Tasian Culture* (London; 1937).

[3] So Baumgärtel, *op. cit.*, p. 26.

of hunting, fowling, fishing, and collecting were of almost equal importance in the provision of food as farming at Merimde and in the Fayum, and scarcely less so in the Badarian and Amratian. Thereafter farming becomes the dominant concern of most Egyptian primary producers. By Early Dynastic times hunting had become a royal sport, but fishing was of course important at all times.

(2) While a variety of handicrafts were plied even in Tasian and Badarian times, none need have engaged full-time specialists. Flint was first mined in the Amratian[1] phase, and that presumably means inter-communal specialization, but the flint-miners need not have been full-time specialists any more than were those of England in Stage IA. Copper was worked by cold hammering occasionally in the Badarian phase and more often in the Amratian, but it did not require full-time smiths. Such must be assumed to produce the cast metal weapons and exceptional tools found in some Gerzean tombs and regularly established in the Early Dynastic period. But even then they consisted mainly of weapons, craftsmen's tools, and luxury articles; for their work in the fields, and even for quarrying and in building, the peasantry and the masses had to make shift with a " Neolithic " equipment of home-made stone, bone, and wood implements. Even metals were not won mainly by communities of full-time miners; the copper lodes of Sinai, for example, were exploited by periodical expeditions sent from the Nile valley and recruited from agricultural families that would normally support themselves by subsistence farming.

During Gerzean and Semainian times the variety of crafts continued to multiply till by Early Dynastic the list of specialists would be longer than that given for Late Helladic Greece or Middle Minoan Crete. But most were

[1] Baumgärtel, *loc. cit.*

employed by the king (pharaoh) and then by his feudal nobles.

(3) The Nile is a moving road providing a relatively economical means of transport even for bulky articles. Boats suitable for river navigation are represented already in the Badarian; they were propelled by paddles. Sailing-boats are first depicted on Semainian scenes, and these are of a new type.[1] Sea-going ships must have been known in Early Dynastic times. On land the ass may have been used as a pack-animal as early as the Amratian, and it is certainly attested at the beginning of Early Dynastic. But wheeled vehicles were not used till fifteen hundred years later, and then at first only as war-chariots.

(4) Luxury imports in the shape of marine shells, beads of coloured stone, and aromatic woods are found already in the Fayum settlements and in Badarian graves. The number and variety of such imports and the distances from which they must have come increase steadily in the sequel; lapis lazuli, for instance, began to reach Egypt presumably from Badakshan in northern Afghanistan in the Gerzean. Actual manufactures imported ready-made from abroad— pottery vases from Palestine or Syria and stone vases from the Ægean—are not recorded before the Early Dynastic. But some earlier works, admittedly executed in Egypt— Gerzean cylinder seals, some Semainian scenes[2] have been interpreted as copies of Mesopotamian originals. By Early Dynastic some sort of regular commerce must have brought Egypt constant supplies of building-timber, spices, metals, and other foreign materials that by then were re-garded as necessities, as well as an increasing array of luxuries.

(5) Weapons—arrows, boomerangs, mace-heads—were

[1] Cf. now also, Winkler, *Rock Drawings of Southern Upper Egypt*, II.

[2] See Dussaud, *Syria,* XVI, p. 332, and Frankfort, *Cylinder Seals* (1939).

regularly deposited in Tasian, Badarian, and Amratian graves. But they could have been used by hunters rather than by warriors, and that they were so used may be inferred by their disappearance from Gerzean and later private graves. But a few Gerzean graves contained copper knife-daggers that would be serviceable in battle. Actual battle scenes are depicted on Gerzean documents, while representations of victory in war were popular in the Early Dynastic. Fortified settlements are then represented, and written documents attest the institution of a standing army.

(6) The village of Merimde covered about six acres over which were scattered twenty-seven small flimsy huts, not all certainly inhabited simultaneously, and one hundred and twenty-five burials. The Tasian and Badarian villages of middle Egypt were probably agglomerations of comparable size located on the edge of the desert above the floodplain beside wadis that still carried water every year.[1] No later settlement has been fully excavated or cleared, and grave-robbing from prehistoric times onwards has disturbed most cemeteries so much that statistics from them are of little value. But the ruins of the prehistoric settlement at Naqada[2] are known to extend over much more than twenty-five acres, and the attached cemetery comprised 2,200 graves, mostly Amratian and Gerzean. Other settlements may have been on a not very much smaller scale,[3] but little villages must have been much more numerous. In historical times there were county towns besides the capital city, and these must go back to prehistoric

---

[1] Brunton, *The Badarian Civilization* (1929) and *Mostagedda* (1937).

[2] Petrie, *Naqada and Ballas* (1890); the ruins of prehistoric "Falcontown" covered at least 13 acres; Brunton, "The Predynastic Town Site at Hierakonpolis," *Studies Presented to F. Ll. Griffiths,* pp. 272-6.

[3] Baumgärtel, *op. cit.,* p. 36.

times, but their populations cannot be estimated at any time.

(7) In historical times the "nomes" or counties into which the lands of Egypt were divided had as emblems animals, plants, or natural objects like the totems of savage and barbarian clans to-day. Many of these emblems occur already by the Gerzean period, if no earlier. They may well represent the totems—divine ancestors and patrons—of kinship groups which in the Semainian or before had become local groups. At the dawn of history the king or pharaoh was mystically identified with one of these "totems," the Falcon (Horus). Presumably other totems had similarly become incarnate in chiefs before the Horus chief conquered the whole of Egypt, subduing the other totems and their earthly representatives.

(8) Female figurines are found in Merimde and in Badarian graves and reappear in all subsequent periods, but male figures occur also in the Amratian[1] and later, while some of the females of that age are carrying pitchers —as if they were slaves and not Mother Goddesses. In historical times goddesses and gods both figured in the Egyptian pantheon, but the dynastic god was at all times male.

Burials of a man and woman in the same grave have been recorded only once from the Badarian period[1] and only rarely from the Amratian.[2] The queens of two very early pharaohs, Zer and Zet,[3] were buried in the same chamber as their lords and presumably at the same time, but one earlier (Merneith, wife of Zer)[4] and all later queens

---

[1] Brunton, *Mostagedda,* p. 44.

[2] Randall-MacIver and Mace, *El Amrah* (1902), graves H.29 and 50 (in H.29 the female corpse occupied the central position!); Ayrton and Loat, *Mahasna* (1911), graves b.17 and 143.

[3] Reisner, *Development of the Egyptian Tomb* (1936), p. 121.

[4] *A.J.A.,* xLVI (1947), p. 192; she was accompanied by artisans with their tools.

were buried in their own tombs with the same distinctive rites as the kings. The pharaohs were from the first polygamous, as were the nobles, at least subsequently, but the queen was normally her husband's sister—a practice confined to the royal family.

(9) Figures scratched on Amratian pots are usually interpreted as proprietary marks indicating private ownership of the vessels and presumably their contents. From Gerzean times seals were thus used to secure ownership. Hunting-dogs were sometimes buried with their masters in the Amratian period, so presumably this means of production was even then personally owned. Models of cattle from graves of the same period would indicate personal ownership of livestock if the models be regarded as magical substitutes for the real oxen. A house model from a Gerzean grave would, on the same assumption, indicate private ownership of dwellings.

Granaries in the Fayum were all grouped together beside the fields at some distance from the settlements. But at Merimde granaries were grouped in the courtyard of each hut, as if the produce of the fields were owned individually by the several families, and this was apparently the practice in later times. But as the annual inundation obliterated all landmarks, village lands had to be redistributed every year among the cultivating families. But in historical times all cultivable land was "owned" by the pharaoh, who however assigned estates, with the cultivators who worked them, to individuals, alive or dead.

Boats depicted on Gerzean vases bear the totemic emblems of counties. Hence on the hypothesis mentioned in para. 7 they may have been communally owned by the several clans or individually by the clan chief as representative of the clan. The pharaoh seems to have "owned" the earliest sea-going ships.

(10) Even in Badarian cemeteries some graves are more

richly furnished than others. Differences in wealth of grave-goods become more marked in subsequent periods and are combined with degrees in the elaboration of the grave itself. But even in Semainian times differences in furniture and construction are gently graduated, so that one hesitates to select any class of graves as those of chiefs contrasted to commoners. But right from the start of the Early Dynastic period the tombs of the first pharaohs stand out at once as royal tombs contrasted to all others, not only in size and construction and in the extravagant wealth buried in them, but also by the immolation of human victims. Observed already under the first two pharaohs, this practice culminated under Zer and Zet, who were accompanied to the tombs by all the harem and household officials to a total of sixty-eight persons in the case of Zer and perhaps one hundred and twenty-three in the tomb of Zet.[1] In the sequel living human beings were replaced by statuettes or other magical devices. High officials or nobles, too, were granted by the early pharaohs the right and the means to build them tombs on the same plan, some exceptionally furnished with a couple of human attendants also. These tombs are, however, easily distinguishable from royal tombs and from the poor pit-graves of commoners.

Thus by the Early Dynastic period Egyptian society is sharply divided into classes—on the one hand pharaoh and a relatively small circle of officials and courtiers, on the other the peasant masses. And it is in the royal tombs that the first written documents occur. As Reisner[2] says, " The needs of the first administration controlling the whole land would have forced the invention of a system of writing." Thus civilization and the unification of Egypt in a single monarchy coincide.

Now, recorded traditions, with which the archæological

[1] See note 2, p. 142.   [2] *Op. cit.*, p. 5.

evidence available fully accords, relate that the unification of Egypt was the consequence of the conquest of the North by a king of the South, leader of the Falcon clan, with its capital at Abydos. Previously there would have been two kingdoms and two lines of kings. But these earlier, pre-pharaonic kings are unsubstantial figures in the archæological as in the literary record—a couple of very archaic inscribed monuments and some tombs at Abydos tentatively attributed by Reisner to Dynasty O alone give substance to the prehistoric kingdom of Upper Egypt. That makes it hard to say how far the unique position of pharaoh in—or rather above—Egyptian society was the fruit of military victory.

Pharaoh was of course a god.[1] But his prehistoric ancestors may have acquired divinity as incarnations of the totem. There is, however, at present no sort of archæological evidence for such an incarnation—for the monopoly of economic as well as spiritual power by an individual member of the clan—before Dynasty O. But these shadowy pre-pharaonic kings must already be " kings of Upper Egypt " as well as chiefs of the Falcon clan. That clan had already attained supremacy, presumably by military prowess, in Upper Egypt before its chief became a king. Hence, as far as archæological evidence goes, it was only when one local or kinship group had secured a military and political hegemony over its neighbours that its leader, whatever his former status, acquired those powers, at once spiritual and economic, that made him and his heirs concretely recognizable as chieftains or gods. Only then did the divine king begin to concentrate the wealth that made civilization possible and writing necessary.

(11) Slavery is not attested in the archæological record in prehistoric Egypt. Even in early historical times, though Nubians and captives were employed as slaves,

[1] Cf. Moret, *The Nile and Egyptian Civilization* (1927).

such slaves were not really important in Egyptian economy. But in the latter period the written sources, the actual products of human labour, and still better the vivid pictures in the tombs, reveal the existence of a huge labour force disciplined by the overseer's lash and employed in quarrying and transporting stone, building tombs and palaces, mining, manufacturing utensils, vases, ornaments, and luxury articles, specialized agriculture, and domestic service for pharaoh and his nobles. These workers were almost certainly not in general full-time specialists, working for wages—i.e., supported entirely' from the social surplus concentrated by pharaoh. Though probably fed and clothed by their employer while employed by him— this is proved by inscriptions in the second millennium— most were recruited from the peasantry either for part of each year or for a term of years; for the rest of their lives they would support themselves by farming land. They were in fact serfs of a kind, but serfdom here must not be interpreted in too legalistic a way. They owed services in return for the right of cultivating land, but no legal machinery existed, or was needed, to prevent them from running away—to the desert, where they were free to starve.

We can guess how this system arose, though we cannot document the hypothetical stages of its development. The exploitation of the Nile valley required exceptionally close social co-operation. Every year the fertilizing flood obliterated the cultivation and might wash away houses and livestock. Every year the land had to be reconquered from desert and marsh. Accordingly, every able-bodied member of each community must participate in digging canals and protective dykes to control the floods, drain the marshes, and distribute the essential water. Such labour was as obligatory and voluntary as military service. To barbarians, work on the construction of houses for gods or fetishes would seem just as necessary and would be just as natural as offerings of "first fruits" or the payment of tithes on the produce of agriculture, hunting, or fishing. Now, in so far as a human leader or chief came to incarnate the totem and to personify society, work for him would be indistinguishable from work for the whole community or its divine ancestor and deity. Whatever process, therefore, had made the pharaoh a god also gave him the moral right to the services of his people as well as to their surplus produce. And he could, and would automatically, confer the same right on those to whom he delegated the execution of his divine functions—the administration of his earthly estate.

Thus under Egyptian conditions the voluntary co-operation of barbarian clansmen could pass over by insensible stages into the corvée—compulsory labour for the personified State and its high officials.

CHAPTER XI

Culture Sequences in Barbarism: (4) Mesopotamia

Unlike the Nile, the Tigris and Euphrates flow through a broad plain sloping gently southwards from the foothills of the Armenian and Iranian mountains. And only the lower courses of the two rivers, when their channels have already come close together, traverse really rainless desert. In northern Mesopotamia—Syria and Assyria—a broad belt immediately south of the mountain ranges enjoys sufficient winter rain to ensure good grass in spring and normally to water cereal crops. Moreover this belt, extending from the Anti-Lebanon and Amanus ranges to the foot of the Iranian plateau, is traversed not only by the great navigable rivers but also by tributary streams—the Balikh, the Khabur, and the Jaghjagha feeding the Euphrates, and the two Zabs and the Diyala flowing into the Tigris from the north-east. As with the Nile, the lower reaches of the twin rivers, swollen by their tributaries, flow through a tract—Babylonia—that would be lifeless but for their annual inundations. But it is still a wide and marshy plain not closely hemmed in by abrupt cliffs.

Northern Mesopotamia is accordingly a steppe, once not even treeless, as to-day.[1] Here the brief winters are really cold, with snow and heavy frosts. Even in northern Babylonia—the ancient Akkad—the winter frosts are severe. Only in southern Babylonia, once termed Sumer (or in the Bible Shinar), is the climate more typically tropical. There the date-palm grows wild luxuriantly, offering a reliable harvest of highly nutritive fruit. Syria and Assyria, with

---

[1] Mallowan, *Iraq,* IX (1947), p. 10.

the adjacent foothills, were, on the contrary, a suitable habitat for wild cereals, fruit-trees, and vines. Species of sheep ancestral to domestic breeds still run wild on the surrounding hills, while wild asses or onagers used to graze upon the steppe.

Successive layers in numerous tells illustrate in exceptional detail stages in the transition from barbarism to civilization. But their builders were completely sedentary farmers acquainted from the first with metal, if not with metallurgy. Earlier stages or cultural periods that an archæologist could label Mesolithic or Neolithic are represented only at a couple of sites[1] yielding hints, too scattered and fragmentary as yet to be relevant to the present inquiry. The available section of the archæological record[2] is divisible into four consecutive "cultures," which also represent consecutive periods of time, named after typical sites—Halaf, al' Ubaid, Uruk, and Jemdet Nasr—and immediately followed in Babylonia by the first phase of literate civilization, termed the Early Dynastic. The first or Halafian culture extends from the Mediterranean coasts of Syria right across to Assyria, and something analogous has recently been recognized also in Sumer on the former shores of the Persian Gulf at Eridu, but it is best represented in the tells along the Balikh, the Khabur, and the Tigris in Assyria. The al' Ubaid culture is as well represented in Sumer as in the north. But the succeeding stages of Uruk and Jemdet Nasr only reached their classical form, which alone is considered in the sequel, in Lower Mesopotamia (Babylonia), where farming and any other form of life depended on the rivers.

(1) The rural economy of the Halafian group was based

[1] Tell Hassuna in Assyria (Lloyd and Safar, *J.N.E.S.*, IV, 1945) and earlier sites discovered by Braidwood in 1948.

[2] For a summary down to 1934 see Childe, *New Light on the Most Ancient East*; to 1949, Perkins, *The Comparative Archæology of Early Mesopotamia* (Chicago).

on the cultivation of cereals and the breeding of cattle, sheep, and pigs from permanent village settlements. As the sites are lined along the marshy valleys of streams and rivers, it is likely that irrigation, natural or artificial, was relied upon to water the crops of cereals and quite possibly orchards and vineyards too. Fishing, collecting, and hunting were certainly important. In the sequel farming, in Lower Mesopotamia at least, must have depended entirely on irrigation. By Early Dynastic times extensive canals had already been dug to spread the waters, to drain the swamps, and even to serve as waterways, but the stages in this development cannot yet be more narrowly defined. It is, however, certain that by Uruk times ploughs were used for tilling the fields.[1]

Literary records disclose the existence of more pastoral groups side by side with the farmers settled in villages or cities. But the relevant texts are scarcely older than 2000 B.C. and such communities are not represented in the archæological record. So we really do know how early this separation of pastoral tribes may have begun in Mesopotamia.

(2) The perfection of pottery and other products of Halafian handicrafts has suggested that already specialized potters, lapidaries, and others were established in each village, but this is uncertain. Intercommunal specialization may, however, be inferred from the extensive use of obsidian in most Halafian villages and the existence of an Halafian village on the site of the nearest natural occurrence of that mineral near Lake Van. Copper was probably known to the Halafians, but most likely only as native metal and for trinkets, so that smiths need not be postulated. Such, however, were engaged in the al' Ubaid period in casting useful axes and other utensils. But the al' Ubaid metal-

[1] Represented as a script character, Falkenstein, *Archäische Texte aus Uruk* (Leipzig; 1936).

lurgists may well have been perambulating smiths, such as we infer for barbarian Europe in Stage IIIB; there is no more evidence for resident craftsmen in al' Ubaid than in Halafian times. In the Uruk period, however, the wheel, operated by professional potters, came into use throughout Mesopotamia, while, particularly in Sumer, metallurgy and other handicrafts must have been separated from agriculture. Indeed, before the end of Uruk times professional clerks were writing accounts in Sumer, and written documents of the Early Dynastic period[1] list coppersmiths, carpenters, silversmiths, sculptors, tanners, spinners, engravers, brewers, bakers, and others as receiving wages or rations from the temples.

(3) As in Egypt, the rivers of Mesopotamia were moving roads, and in historical times the great canals of Babylonia were almost as important for transport as for irrigation. Boats are represented by models as early as the al' Ubaid phase, and were probably already propelled by sails as well as paddles.[2] But on the wide plain land transport was naturally more necessary than in the narrow valley of the Nile, while the open steppe between the rivers is easily negotiable. Horses or asses are frequently depicted on Halafian vases,[3] but it is by no means certain whether the beasts were tame and used for transport. Nor is the use of wheeled vehicles certain at this stage, though the design on one broken vase has been interpreted as a representation of some sort of wheeled vehicle. Such were demonstrably in use, together with sledges, as early as the Uruk period,[4] when war-chariots also seem to be represented. Sleds and carts were drawn by oxen, but chariots by onagers and perhaps sometimes by horses[5] from the Jemdet Nasr phase

[1] Deimel, " Sumerische Tempelwirtschaft zur Zeit Urukaginas," *Analacta Orientalia*, 2 (Rome; 1931).
[2] *Sumer*, IV (1948), p. 118.
[3] Mallowan, *Iraq*, IX, p. 13.   [4] See note 1, p. 150.
[5] At Chagar Bazar, Mallowan, *Iraq*, III (1936), p. 10.

onwards. Pack-asses may be assumed by this period, and are frequently mentioned in later documents.

(4) The distribution of obsidian from Armenia had begun in Assyria even before the Halafian period, and the material reached even Sumer in considerable quantities in al' Ubaid times. Conversely, shells from the Persian Gulf were transported to the Khabur valley of North Syria by the Halafian phase. Then, too, at least small trinkets of copper were being imported, and in the al' Ubaid phase the metal was reaching Sumer in sufficient quantities to be used for tools and weapons, though in fact only clay models of copper axes and knives survive.[1] By the Uruk period regular supplies of this metal and also of lead, silver, and gold had been established. Conversely, seals in Jemdet Nasr style must have reached Turkey, Egypt, and the Ægean, where they were copied.[2] In early historical times it is known that metals were imported into Sumer from Oman on the Persian Gulf and from the Turkish plateau (Anatolia), and it seems reasonably certain that this long-distance trade was established in Jemdet Nasr, if not also in Uruk, times. Similarly, lapis lazuli, derived from northern Afghanistan, reached Sumer as early as the Jemdet Nasr period and was imported in quite large quantities in Early Dynastic times. Of course, the lapis lazuli brought to Egypt (p. 138) presumably came from the same source and must therefore have travelled through Mesopotamia. Babylonia was accordingly becoming a centre for long-distance international trade even in prehistoric times. By the Early Dynastic period not only were raw materials like metals, timber from Lebanon or Amanus, and stone from Oman being imported into Babylonia, but even seals and ornaments manufactured by

[1] The best come from Uqair, *J.N.E.S.*, II (1943), Pls. XVI, *b* and XVIII.

[2] Frankfort, *Cylinder Seals* (London; 1939), p. 232.

urban craftsmen far away in the valley of the Indus.[1] Later on the literary records show that manufactures of the Babylonian textile industries were being exported to the Turkish plateau in exchange for metals, and a similar export of manufactures must be assumed for late prehistoric and Early Dynastic times.

Professional merchants[2] are mentioned in some of the earliest decipherable documents and must be assumed at least as early as the Uruk period. The frequent exchanges then attested must have required the social recognition of standards of weights, and sure enough hæmatite weights already occur, while the written documents from the end of the period illustrate the use of standard measures of volume for liquids and probably also for cereals. The units of weight seem to have been based at the start on measures of barley, and weighed quantities of this grain also formed standards of value. But by Early Dynastic times weighed quantities of silver formed the standard for all important transactions. Beyond this translation of a cereal into a metallic standard of value Mesopotamian societies advanced no further towards the creation of coined currency within our period.

(5) Halafian settlements seem to have been unfortified, and the only weapons found in them are sling-stones, more suitable for the hunter than for the warrior. But by the al' Ubaid period some axes of stone or copper look more like "battle-axes" than tools.[3] In any case by Uruk times fortified cities and battle-scenes, in which chariots and bound captives figure, are depicted on seals. At the dawn of history Babylonia was divided into a number of auto-

[1] Oriental Institute, Chicago, *Communications,* 16 (1933), p. 47; 19 (1935), p. 53; and Gadd, *Proc. British Academy,* XVIII.

[2] Schneider, *Die Sumerische Tempelstadt* (*Staatwissenschaftl. Beiträge,* IV) (Essen; 1920), pp. 62-6.

[3] The best come from Uqair, *J.N.E.S.,* II (1943), Pls. XVI, *b* and XVIII.

nomous city-States, frequently at war with one another. Citizen soldiers were armed with copper axes, spears, daggers, and helmets, and were disciplined to fight in phalanx formation. At the same time chariots drawn by onagers or horses were employed as engines of war,[1] though it is not certain that they played such a decisive military, and therefore also sociological, role as for instance in Late Helladic Greece (p. 182).

Some quite early texts refer to " expeditions " sent out by city-States to obtain metal, stone, or other raw materials,[2] but it is really very doubtful whether much of the supplies needed for urban industry and armament was obtained as booty or tribute.

(6) The typical settlement sites throughout North Syria and Assyria are now marked by oval mounds varying in size from 400 m. × 300 m. (435 × 330 yards) to 230 m. × 150 m. (250 × 164 yards.)[3] None has been so completely excavated or published that the total built-up area can be accurately estimated at any given period. The larger figure quoted (equivalent to say thirty acres) refers to a settlement not occupied after the Halaf period, but normal villages in the historical period in this region do not form larger mounds. In southern Mesopotamia, however, the fortified areas in Early Dynastic times were much greater: Khafaje on the Divala[4] covered one hundred acres, Ur[5] two hundred and twenty acres, Erech[6] perhaps two square miles. Even in prehistoric times the unit of

---

[1] All illustrated on the standard from Ur often reproduced.
[2] Schneider, *Die Sumerische Tempelstadt* (*Staatwissenschaftl. Beiträge,* IV) (Essen; 1920), pp. 62-6.
[3] Mallowan, *Iraq,* viii (1946), 123 ff.
[4] Delougaz, *The Oval Temple at Khafaje,* Oriental Institute *Publication,* LIII (1941), p. 137.
[5] Woolley, *Ant. J.,* IX (1929), pp. 336-7. For estimates of actual population see Frankfort, *Kingship and the Gods* (1948), p. 96, n. 23.
[6] *Abhandl. preuss. Akad., phil. hist.,* KL (1935), No. 4.

settlement on the plain may have been larger than on the northern steppe. No exact figures are indeed available, but a single temple of the al' Ubaid period at Eridu[1] in Sumer covered 77 by 39 feet (337 square yards), while one chapel at Gawra[2] in Assyria of the same period measured over all only 57 by 43 feet—it was, however, one of three shrines which, with a central court, covered together 717 square yards. At the close of the Uruk phase, on the other hand, a single temple at Erich [3] measured 245 by 100 feet over all. On the whole there is therefore no evidence that the earlier settlements in Sumer were substantially larger than those on the steppe zone farther north, but a radical expansion must have begun in the next, the Uruk period.

(7) Even at Hassuna,[4] a settlement earlier than the Halafian culture, the houses consisted of several rooms grouped round a central court, and this remained a normal fashion, as it is indeed to-day. There is no need to assume that such houses were occupied by any group larger than the " natural family." That does not of course mean that a Mesopotamian village was just an aggregate of unrelated households. On the contrary, at the beginning of history we find most even of the citizens of Lagash divided into a score of divine households and styled respectively the " people of Baü " or of some other of the twenty deities.

(8) Figurines of women occur before the Halafian period and continue to be made in all subsequent ages. In historical times some such figures undoubtedly represent Ishtar or some other goddess, but by that time gods, too, were worshipped and the family was normally patriarchal, both among the gods and on earth. In fact even in the al' Ubaid phase a few exceptional figurines represent males.

[1] *Sumer*, III, pt. 2 (Baghdad; 1947).
[2] *Bull. American School Oriental Research*, 66 (1937); Perkins, op. cit., pp. 65-9.
[3] *Abhandl. preuss. Akad., phil. hist.*, KL (1933).
[4] *J.N.E.S.*, IV (1945), pp. 272 ff.

In al' Ubaid times a few graves contain the bodies of men and women buried together. In one grave of this period at Arpachiya[1] the bodies were locked in an embrace, but in the large cemetery at Eridu[2] successive interments in the same grave have been observed.

(9) Even in the pre-Halafian village of Hassuna grain was stored in the houses, as if the produce of the fields was the private property of the household that cultivated them. In the Halafian period seals were impressed on the clay stoppers of jars, as if to denote proprietary rights in their contents. In the Uruk period cylinders began to replace stamp seals. But even at the beginning of the historical period most of the land round a city like Lagash[3] was owned by a deity, though it was allotted for use individually to the "god's people." The deity also owned metal tools, ploughs, and plough-animals for use in its cultivation, though it is not certain that individual allotment-holders might not also have owned such instruments of production. At this time some craftsmen probably owned their own tools, but they did not normally own stocks of raw materials nor manufacture for the market, but worked to order on material supplied by the customer. The only "customer," at least for metal-ware, actually recorded at this time was the deity or the "State." Even merchants acted as agents for the deity and had shares in the deity's land, but they seem already to have been able to make a private profit. On the other hand, town land with buildings on it may already have been privately owned and capable of alienation by sale or bequest.

(10) Even in the Halafian villages of the northern steppe zone[4] one building already stands out from all the rest by its size and plan as a shrine or temple. So in the al'

---

[1] *Iraq,* II, p. 39.   [2] *Sumer,* IV (1948), p. 117.

[3] Deimel, *Sumerische Tempelwirtschaft,* p. 79.

[4] Speiser, "Closing the Gap at Tepe Gawra," *Asia* (1938), p. 536; cf. Perkins, *op. cit.,* p. 40.

Ubaid period in Sumer the principal edifice at Eridu was a temple, repeatedly rebuilt on an ever more grandiose scale, till in form and size it conforms to the familiar outlines of the historical Sumerian temple. Before the end of the Uruk period such temples in Sumer, but not in Syria or Assyria, had already reached the truly monumental proportions mentioned on p. 153. Plainly the erection and plenishing of such fanes presupposes the existence of a substantial social surplus and its concentration in the hands of the deity. Now, at the beginning of written history we find the temple already staffed and administered by a corporation of priests and enriched not only by the free-will offerings but by the tithes and services of the god's people who held shares in the god's land or worked it as tenants or sharecroppers.

Thus the temple by the Uruk period had demonstrably become, and had been inferentially much earlier, a centre for the accumulation of the social surplus. It was in order to keep account of the receipts and expenditure of the deity that the priestly corporations administering the temple estate devised and sanctioned a system of conventional signs—i.e., of writing; the only written documents of the Uruk and Jemdet Nasr periods are in fact account tablets or lists of signs. Thus the accumulation of a substantial social surplus in the temple treasuries—or rather granaries —was actually the occasion of the cultural advance that we have taken as the criterion of civilization. At the same time it made possible other advances; for the concentrated surplus was used not only to support priests, some of whom had leisure to devise writing and then elaborate sciences of arithmetic and astronomy, but also various artisans and craftsmen, like spinners and weavers, some of whose manufactures were exported to obtain metal and other requisite raw materials.

The deity may be regarded as a representative or projection of the community, and the priests who served him would therefore be servants of the community, though doubtless better paid than the rest of the god's people. Till Jemdet Nasr times we have no positive indication of any secular authority concentrating economic and political power. Then, however, we meet buildings that look more like a palace than a temple, while from Early Dynastic times archæological and literary evidence reveals a civil governor and military leader in each city.

This ruler bore various titles in different cities—*lugal,* "war lord"; *sangu,* "temple administrator"; *en,* "spouse of the city goddess"; or most often *ishakku* or *ensi.* Jacobsen[1] has adduced literary evidence to show that the position of leader in war had been originally elective, but at the dawn of written history the office of city governor seems to have been in practice hereditary. Yet the governor was always closely associated with the temple, and in extant inscriptions he confesses that he is but the servant or vicegerent of the city god (who was himself the community writ large). Yet at Lagash the *ishakku,* who was also high priest of Ningirsu, the chief god, controlled in the latter capacity the sole urban granary and so the food supply of the urban population; no granaries were attached to the temples of the remaining deities, who otherwise owned estates and households, as did Ningirsu himself. But in pure theory the city governor was servant of the city god as well as all other citizens. It was only when one city began to obtain hegemony over others by military conquest that the governor of the victorious city came to exercise over subjects—at first the inhabitants of conquered cities—lordship at all comparable to that enjoyed by the first pharaohs.

(11) The first decipherable documents of Early Dynastic

[1] "Primitive Democracy in Ancient Mesopotamia," *J.N.E.S.,* 11 (1943), p. 159.

times mention farmers holding shares, of varying sizes, in the god's land; tenants working it as sharecroppers; free labourers employed as cultivators or in other capacities for wages; and slaves. Probably even the first classes were bound to perform labour service for the maintenance of canals and the construction of temples just as much as military service, and in prehistoric times it may be assumed the same customary services secured the labour power requisite for the building of the temples that have actually been discovered and of the canals that can confidently be assumed. At least from the Uruk period pictures survive of bound captives who presumably were kept as slaves. But it is not at all likely that slaves and captives formed an important element in the labour force engaged on public works.

CHAPTER XII

Conclusions

The last five chapters have summarized in a very abstract way successive steps through which barbarian cultures actually passed on the road to civilization in contrasted natural environments. Let us compare them to see whether they exhibit uniformity or parallelism and whether they represent general stages on the route.

Of course, the final result—civilization—was concretely very different in each case. Yet everywhere it did mean the aggregation of large populations in cities; the differentiation within these of primary producers (fishers, farmers, etc.), full-time specialist artizans, merchants, officials, priests, and rulers; an effective concentration of economic and political power; the use of conventional symbols for recording and transmitting information (writing), and equally conventional standards of weights and of measures of time and space leading to some mathematical and calendrical science. The starting point, too, in each series was, rather less abstractly, similar—at least in the economic sphere—inasmuch as all the first barbarian cultures examined were based on the cultivation of the same cereals and the breeding of the same species of animals.

But the intervening steps in development do not exhibit even abstract parallelism. Consider rural economy. In Tasian and Badarian Egypt farming was at best on a par with, and perhaps even subordinate to, the food-gathering activities of hunting, fishing, and collecting; in the sequel the relative importance of hunting rapidly declined. In temperate Europe we saw just the reverse: in Central and

Western Europe hunting was relatively less important in Neolithic Stage I than in the succeeding Stage II (p. 108). Again, in Greece as well as in Hither Asia and Egypt the first definable rural economy was organized so as to permit of really sedentary farming—i.e., the continuous exploitation of a tract of land from a permanent village or hamlet. In temperate Europe shifting cultivation was the rule throughout the Neolithic and most of the Bronze stages. (It is of course self-evident that this contrast must involve quite radical divergences in the whole structure of the societies concerned.) In the last-named area we observed a separation of more pastoral from more agricultural communities; nothing parallel was disclosed by archæology in Egypt or Mesopotamia. (In the last-named province it is attested by written evidence, but only some time after civilization had emerged.)

So the observed developments in rural economy do not run parallel; they cannot therefore be used to define stages common to all the sequences examined. No doubt in the Old World plough cultivation had everywhere replaced hoe cultivation before the rise of civilization. But it is fair to recall that the plough was unknown to the civilized Mayas, who had in fact no domestic animals at all. Hence the plough could not be used to define a necessary stage on the road to civilization even if its age in the several Old World regions were accurately defined. In fine, the development of barbarians' rural economies in the regions surveyed exhibits not parallelism but divergence and convergence. The divergences may be adequately explained by saying that what archæology reveals is the adaptation of one rural economy to different natural environments. To the phenomenon of convergence we must return later.

Chapter II has already shown why the technological criteria currently used by archæologists—the materials employed for cutting-tools and weapons—cannot provide serviceable bases for defining general stages in cultural evolution. A careful perusal of the last chapters will have shown how very diverse were the modes in which metal was used during, say, the Early Bronze Age. It now appears, too, that means of transport are no more serviceable; in Crete and temperate Europe as well as in Hither Asia wheeled vehicles were in use before civilization was achieved, but on the Nile such were unknown for one thousand five hundred years after the foundation of civilization. Here again we have divergence rather than parallelism, but in the Old World this divergence was rectified later by convergence; Egypt did in the end adopt the chariot.

External trade does indeed illustrate the sort of parallelism we have been seeking, since its volume and extent did increase continually in all the zones studied. But this parallelism is not very helpful, after all. On the one hand, it is impossible, with the data available, to measure foreign trade at all precisely. On the other hand, in so far as it is measurable, it turns out that in temperate Europe and even in the Ægean the first major increases were in commerce with civilization—i.e., with regions where a substantial social surplus had already been accumulated. To that extent the observed growth in trade would be a function not of the internal development of the barbarian societies concerned but of their social environment—i.e., of their relations with other societies.

The fragmentary record of the development of social institutions in the several sequences, in so far as it is decipherable at all, suggests no closer parallelism. In Egypt and Crete and among the Celts in temperate Europe civilization was preceded by the rise of chiefs to the status of divine kings who concentrate the social surplus. In Mesopotamia, on the contrary, it was the temple of a superhuman divinity that performed this function, and did it so effectively that writing had to be invented and civilization thus sealed in the Uruk phase; first in the succeeding Jemdet Nasr phase may a presumed palace indicate the rule of an earthly prince, while "royal tombs," the usual archæological indications of such personages, are recognizable only later still, near the end of the Early Dynastic phase. It was not in fact till the "Imperial Age" after 2350 B.C. that a Mesopotamian king appears in the literary record invested with anything like the authority and divinity which a pharaoh enjoyed from the foundation of Egyptian civilization.

In the Ægean, while there had been in the barbarian Bronze Age "kings" endowed in their minute domains with the same sort of majesty and function as an Oriental monarch, in most, but not all, Greek States these had been replaced by "republican" oligarchies of landowners or merchants before civilization was actually established. (This discrepancy was in the long run compensated for by the Hellenistic monarchies and then by the Roman Empire.) Even among the Celts in temperate Europe the sort of kingship illustrated by the late Hallstatt and early La Tène barrows had waned before the Roman conquest; the conquerors generally had to deal with more or less "republican" States.

Whether all or indeed any of the barbarian societies here considered started on the road to civilization under the rule of chiefs or as "primitive democracies" the archæological record leaves in doubt. At least in Central Europe chieftainship seems to be excluded in the case of the earliest recognizable Neolithic society—the Danubians at Köln-Lindenthal. On the other hand, in Western Europe Megalithic tombs and long barrows may conceivably represent chieftains' family vaults. And in Chapter VI we adduced positive evidence for the institution in societies that had not reached the status of barbarism at all—but the most reliable cases came from societies that were not so extremely ancient that influence from barbarian neighbours could be excluded.

Similar ambiguities encompass the institution of war. All known civilized societies engaged in this destructive pursuit. On the contrary, some early Neolithic barbarians, like the Danubians, have left a definitely peaceful impression. Yet the first farmers in Northern Europe carried warlike weapons, and those of Western Europe fortified their settlements in England. Moreover, homicide and cannibalism are well attested among Palæolithic savages (p. 80).

As for the position of women, the same sort of evidence as is taken to indicate monogamy and *sati* (implying the subordination of females to males) in the Bronze Age societies of Greece and temperate Europe is available in savage vultures from the Mesolithic of the Crimea (p. 53) to the belated Stone Age of Siberia. So on the whole archæology does not hold out much prospect of correlating social institutions with stages of cultural development as defined in economic terms. But, after all, we have seen that such stages, apart from the three main status, are themselves hard, if not impossible to define. For within the status of barbarism at least, the observable cultural sequences do not follow parallel lines.

Now, it is not in the least surprising that the development of societies observed in different parts of the Old World, to say nothing of the New, should exhibit divergence rather than parallelism. This conclusion does not invalidate the use of the term "evolution" to describe social development, nor even the implied analogy between social and organic evolution. To Lamarck and Darwin "evolution" described a process by which new species emerged—that is to say, a process of variation and differentiation. Organic evolution is never represented pictorially by a bundle of parallel lines, but by a tree with branches all up the trunk and each branch bristling with twigs. In so far as the archæological picture could be represented by such a figure, it would disclose a process analogous to organic evolution. In fact, differentiation—the splitting of large homogeneous cultures into a multitude of distinct local cultures—is a conspicuous feature in the archæological record.

But a comparison of the sequences summarized discloses not only divergence and differentiation, but also convergence and assimilation. To the latter phenomena it is hard to find an analogy in organic evolution. No doubt natural selection brings about assimilation in a given area by the elimination of many varieties within one species or genus. When several genetically different groups of the same species are competing for the limited natural resources of a given region, the best-adapted group will in time eliminate all competitors. To this sort of process there are of course prehistoric, as well as historic, analogies among human societies or cultures. In prehistoric Europe, for instance, we have seen that the Beaker culture replaced the Western Neolithic A in Britain; throughout the island the rural economy and burial rites of the latter vanished utterly to make room for those of the Beaker culture. That is clearly the counterpart of recorded cases in which one people or tribe exterminate or enslave another and occupy their territory, as Europeans have occupied Australia and North America.

But such total replacement of one society or culture by another is not the typical form of convergence and not that generally observed to lead to civilization. Two cultures may become more alike without losing their distinctive individualities. The same novelty may appear simultaneously in two distinct cultures, or first in one and then in another; both consequently become more alike. So, for instance, the cultures of Egypt and Greece became more like those of Hither Asia when their armaments were enriched by the addition of war chariots, used in Mesopotamia a thousand years earlier. Now since a culture is an organic whole, all the elements of which more or less influence all the rest, " more like " in this case means more than saying $A + B + C + X$ is more like $D + E + F + X$ than $A + B + C$ is like $D + E + F$; we really get $Ax + Bx + Cx + X$ and $Dx + Ex + Fx + X$.

In the same way Russia and Japan became more like England and one another when they, too, began to build and use railways. Russian and Japanese railways did not symbolize an English conquest or the suppression of, say, samovars and Orthodox Christianity or of rickshaws and Shintoism. Nor did the chariot in Egypt or Europe symbolize a Babylonian conquest or the suppression of most distinctively Egyptian, Minoan, or Mycenæan institutions, customs, fashions of dress, and styles of art. Nevertheless it is an historical fact that railways were invented in England and were built in Russia in deliberate imitation of English models and indeed under the direction of English engineers. It is almost equally certain that Egyptian chariotry was copied from the Asiatic. The same is probably true of the Cretan and Greek—and in the long run of that adopted in temperate Europe, though there the models would be taken immediately from the Mycenæan Greeks or perhaps the Etruscans.

In both examples we are dealing with cultural borrowing between politically and culturally distinct societies. This is what is termed diffusion. Most cases of assimilation in which the priority of the new common trait in one society is established must be explained by diffusion. Where it is not certain that the new trait was exhibited in one culture earlier than all the rest, the position is more debatable. The possibility of independent invention can never be ruled out *a priori*; in some cases it has to be admitted. In 1950 it certainly seems that pottery appeared in Northern Europe before any Neolithic farmers had advanced far enough north to impart the art to local savages, but yet too late to be the progenitor of Egyptian or Mesopotamian ceramics. If so, the discovery—or rather the discoveries—involved must have been made at least twice. Pottery is usually taken as a crucial case by diffusionists, but of course what applies to inventions or discoveries in material equipment applies at least as fully to innovations in institutions, ritual, and art.

Now, just as convergence distinguishes social from organic evolution, so diffusion is peculiar to social adaptation—that is, to evolution; so diffusion is culture. For of course culture represents the means by which societies adapt themselves to their environments so as to survive and multiply, taking the place of the bodily modifications and instincts that serve animals to the same end. This peculiarity is in turn a function of the way in which culture evolves and is transmitted.

The mechanism of organic evolution whereby new species arise may be summarized roughly as follows: Through unknown causes (we say therefore " by chance " or " at random ") a mutation occurs in one or more genes of an individual of a species. This will be transmitted by sexual reproduction to some of its offspring. If the mutation be beneficial, those who inherit and exhibit the new character will have a better chance of survival than all the rest of the species; they will probably live longer and produce more offspring. After many generations they will have replaced all competitors in a given local population. (If the advantage conferred by new character be of the order of one per cent this replacement will take five hundred generations in a population of a few thousand!) Thus a new species will have been established locally.

Cultural changes take place much more expeditiously. An individual member of a society discovers or invents a new device—or it may be a new pattern, a new song, or a new rite. The discoverer or inventor can immediately impart it by precept and example to other members of his society. If he convince them of its utility or virtue—if, that is, society approves the innovation—it will then be adopted generally by the society, whose culture will be enriched and changed to that extent. A cultural change could thus be established within a human population much more quickly than a mutation in a population of even such a quick-breeding species as mice! For the cultural innovation could be adopted by a whole population in less than one generation. Then all the members of the next generation as they grow up will be taught by their elders to use the new device or practise the new rite, which thus becomes permanently enshrined in the social heritage of the community.

But the process need not stop there. Inventions can be transmitted from one society to another, and that is precisely what diffusion means. But that is just what is impossible in organic evolution. By no possible means can one species transmit to another the mutation which has proved beneficial, even though both inhabit the same region. All that can happen is that natural selection gradually eliminates the species that lacks the mutation. It is, I suggest, the operation of diffusion more than anything else that distinguishes social from organic evolution and explains the curvature of the lines in any graphic representation of the process.

Admittedly not all convergence is to be explained in this way. Admittedly, too, diffusion is hard to prove archæologically. But archæology can prove intercourse—i.e., opportunity for diffusion—between different societies; the transmission of material objects from one group to another by human agency is an observable fact. It has been repeatedly mentioned in the previous chapters under the rubric "trade." The heading "intercourse" might have been used just as well. For as material objects can be transmitted from one community to another, so can ideas, and this transmission can in fact be observed too. Of course, ideas never fossilize. But they may be realized in actions that leave durable impressions on the archæological record. Two examples will suffice to illustrate how the transmission of ideas between societies already shown to have been connected by "trade" can legitimately be inferred.

In Chapter VII it appeared that Neolithic "Danubian" communities in Central Europe by direct or indirect "trade" obtained shells from the Mediterranean. Now, after a time, Danubians in Hungary and Moravia occasionally made curious cubes of clay with a cup-like hollow in the centre of one face and string holes at the corners. It is an absurd shape for a pottery vessel, but reproduces exactly the form of stone paint-pots or unguent vases very popular in Crete, Egypt, and Mesopotamia during the third millennium b.c.—a nice symmetrical shape easily fashioned in stone. It may safely be inferred that the Neolithic Danubians, being unskilled in making stone vases, were copying rather slavishly in pottery the stone paint-pots of the Ægean and the Near East. In other words, they had borrowed the idea from the Orient but translated it into local materials and native techniques.

Secondly, the Egyptians of the Gerzean phase and the Sumerians of Mesopotamia from the Uruk period must have been linked together by "trade," since both were importing lapis lazuli; this substance, being reputedly derived from Afghanistan, must have reached the Nile by way of the Tigris-Euphrates plain. Now, at the close of the Gerzean phase we find Egyptian artists beginning, but continuing only for a short time, to use motives and designs that were already, and long remained, popular in Mesopotamia—animals with heads at both ends of their bodies, monsters with intertwined necks, antithetical groups, and so on. About the same time the same Egyptians began to make cylinder seals and to decorate them with rows of animals as in the case of the Uruk and Jemdet Nasr cylinders of Mesopotamia, though invariably treated in an Egyptian style. The cylinder seal, always used thereafter in Mesopotamia, was practically replaced by older forms of stamp seal in historical Egypt. Here too we must admit that Egyptians adopted Mesopotamian art motives and devices, only to discard them in the sequel.

It would be easy to multiply examples, but the two instances should suffice to show that ideas were actually transmitted from one society to another and in each case adapted to the latter's culture. In both examples the borrowed ideas were subsequently discarded. They were in fact chosen for that reason, since the ultimate rejection of the idea by one party and its retention by the other help materially to sustain the latter's claim to have originated the innovation. But it must not be assumed that rejection was the normal fate of a borrowed device—quite the reverse is true. But the outcome in this case illustrates another significant point. Diffusion is not an automatic process, like infection with a disease. One society can borrow an idea—a technical invention, a political institution, a superstitious rite, or an artistic motive—only when it fits into the general pattern of the society's culture—in other words, when that society has evolved to a stage which allows of the acceptance of the idea.

That is most easily seen in the case of technical advances. The potter's wheel, like the wheeled car, was quite certainly diffused in temperate Europe, but it was only adopted, centuries later than wheeled vehicles, when and where other technical and political developments required or allowed the concentration of population into relatively large aggregates; for, to make a living, a professional potter needs a numerous clientele living fairly close to his workshop. The spread of iron-working indicates a converse case. Though practised in Palestine and the Ægean by 1000 B.C., the new technique and its products were not adopted in the Nile valley till about four hundred years later. Till then the innovation did not satisfy a *socially approved* need of Egyptian culture; long-established economic and political institutions offered a quite unconscious resistance to the use of cheap iron.

The second of our examples proving diffusion of ideas has a further significance. In Egypt and Lower Mesopotamia it was just when intercourse with other societies had become most intense that the pace of cultural change became so fast that we can speak of a revolution—the transition from savagery to civilization. A similar correlation is observable in other societies—in Middle Minoan Crete, in Mycenæan Greece, and in temperate Europe in the La Tène period. Of course, in default of suitable methods of measurement and of adequate data to measure, no exact correlation can be established. Still, the archæological data adduced justify at least the assertion that progressive change is accelerated by intercourse with divergently adapted and differently organized societies.

In any case, the evidence cited leaves no doubt that intercourse went on between the diverse geographical regions where relatively full culture sequences are available throughout the whole period when barbarism reigned in each. That intercourse helps to explain the convergences observed in very diverse natural environments. It also shows why we have failed to define in all regions similar stages, intermediate between barbarism and civilization. For on the one hand the processes of change have been too rapid to allow of the total integration of the societies affected by diffusion into stable new configurations. On the other hand, the several series considered are not in fact so completely independent of one another as to constitute distinct "instances" from which inductions can legitimately be drawn.

This last conclusion, after all, really became at once explicit in our sketch of the development of rural economy in several regions; what archæology seems to disclose are not the independent discoveries and improvements of methods of cultivation and stock-breeding, but rather the adaptation of one and the same complex of discoveries to divergent environments. Hence even in this limited domain we cannot justly say that any community of Neolithic or Bronze Age farmers in Bohemia or Britain was systadial with any one in Crete or Egypt, still less in the Pacific or Africa to-day.

Within the status of savagery, at least in so far as that be confined to Palæolithic and Mesolithic times, the position may have been different; the total human population of the Earth in the Pleistocene and of North-Western Europe in the early Holocene (the archæologists' Mesolithic Age is thus restricted in space as well as time) was so small and scattered that intercourse between groups and regions must have been exceptional. But within those chronological limits the archæological data are still so scanty and ambiguous that no sociological generalizations seem legitimate. By the time the sources supply richer documentation, the possibility of diffusion can no longer be excluded. After all, communication between the Mediterranean coasts and the Dordogne is established for the Miolithic (Upper Palæolithic) and between the Urals and the Baltic for the Mesolithic. So the hunter-fishers on L. Onega (p. 84), whose burials suggested some sort of chieftainship, were contemporary with communities of Neolithic farmers living round the south western Baltic, in South, and perhaps even in Central, Russia; their "savage" social institutions may have been influenced by those of these neighbouring barbarians. For other communities of the same society—i.e., with the same culture—were demonstrably in "commercial" contact with such farmers.

In Siberia again by the Glazkovo phase (p. 85) contact with Bronze Age cultures farther south is explicitly attested by imported manufactures. In the preceding Kitoï phase, which gives the first hints from the region of chieftainship and *sati,* "trade" was already so extensive as to afford opportunities for intercourse over a wide area, and so the possibility of diffusion from more advanced centres.

In fine, then, the analogy between cultural evolution and organic evolution breaks down. But to admit this is not to deny cultural evolution, to deny that cultural change is an orderly and rational process that can be understood by the human intellect without invoking any necessarily incalculable factors and miracles. On the contrary, it can be described in general intelligible formulæ. Indeed, with certain modification the Darwinian formula of "variation, heredity, adaptation, and selection" can be transferred from organic to social evolution, and is even more intelligible in the latter domain than in the former.

In the case of variation, the mechanism of cultural change, invention, is more intelligible than that of its counterpart, mutation. Not only does no one know the cause of the modification in the submicroscopic segment of a chromosome that produces a mutation, no one can predict when it will occur or in what direction. It is also at present impossible to describe precisely how the gene changes and how this change affects the whole organism-to-be. But invention is something that everyone is doing every day—say in devising a substitute for a mislaid corkscrew or composing a really new sentence in an essay.

The mechanism of social heredity is, as explained on p. 169, different from and much more expeditious than biological heredity. But it too is a familiar, intelligible, and, to some degree, controllable process. It is effected by example and precept, by education, advertisement, and propaganda. This process, we repeat, is much more rapid than the biological mechanism of sexual reproduction.

Adaptation to the environment is a condition of survival for societies as much as for organisms. The process can be illustrated from archæology as shown in the discussion of rural economies. But in cultural adaptation the internal social environment is relatively more important than in biology. Cases have already been quoted to show how a new device, however " efficient " from our standpoint, can be adopted by a society only if it satisfies a socially approved want and fits in to the whole cultural pattern. But the process can be much faster in human than in natural history owing to the different methods of transmission. An acquired adaptation—say the musculature of an acrobat—cannot be transmitted to the offspring by biological heredity. But the acrobat may teach his children—and people quite unrelated to him genealogically —the movements and exercises that developed his muscles.

At the same time the environment to which adaptation is required includes other societies. A device or institution, however well adapted to the needs of a given society and its physical environment, will be permanently beneficial only if it help that society to adapt itself to its neighbours. Now, the social environment is much more variable than the material, both because culture changes much faster than climate, or even vegetation, and because cultures spread, whether by migration or by some other form of diffusion. So a society, like an animal species, can become over-specialized, so happily adapted to one particular environment that its culture cannot be adjusted to a sudden change in its environment or cannot even assimilate useful innovations offered by the external social environment. The former disability was illustrated by the Magdalenians' culture in Europe at the end of the Ice Age and has been repeatedly illustrated in history when relatively prosperous barbarian tribes or even civilized peoples like the Aztecs and Incas have been confronted with European civilization. The second case has just been documented by a reference to Egypt at the end of the Bronze Age (p. 169).

The term "selection" can be applied to the mechanism of cultural evolution in only a rather specialized sense as a result of the differences just considered. In the five hundred thousand years of humanity's existence an infinity of innovations must have been attempted or suggested. Owing to a rigorous process of selection, only a fraction have survived as being in the long run beneficial. So far the analogy with the selection of mutations is valid. But the mechanism of selection is quite different.

In the "survival of the fittest" it is first those members of a population who carry the mutation who survive and multiply *at the expense of* those individuals who lack it. And then the new species thus established spreads by *eliminating* other species. Similar selective mechanisms operate within and between societies; the second at least can be seen at work in prehistory as well as in history (p. 162). But both are rather extravagant methods. The first may kill off individuals possessing useful knowledge and potentially still more useful qualities just because they lack some technique or do not conform to some custom that is for the moment socially useful. Their elimination is really unnecessary inasmuch as they can be trained in the desirable technique or educated to observe the necessary custom. Submission to vaccination might have become an established habit in Britain after a series of epidemics had killed off all unvaccinated persons; the habit was established much more rapidly and economically by propaganda and legislation.

On the other hand, to survive at all any culture must be fairly well adapted to its specific environment. If it has to be annihilated to make room for a better-adapted culture, the discoveries and inventions by which the former's adaptation was achieved are liable to be lost altogether. Actually this seldom happens. Even in prehistory, when the change of culture in one region is so abrupt and drastic that we speak of one culture replacing another and infer the conquest of the region by a foreign society, most of the old achievements survive to be incorporated in the new culture. In Middle Helladic Greece, while burial rites, pottery forms, house plans, and some other elements were new, the habit of grouping the houses in towns, metallurgy, navigation, and other techniques, the commercial ties, and presumably the rural economy, survived from the preceding Early Helladic culture. The newcomers had added to the pre-existing material equipment horses and wheeled vehicles. They suppressed collective burial to make room for a new rite, and doubtless changed other political and religious institutions, but retained many intact. The same sort of continuity is observable across the wider gap between Mycenæan and Geometric times. The cultural history of Greece does indeed illustrate selection by elimination, but it discloses still more conspicuously accumulation, and this is distinctive of cultural evolution.

At the same time the spread of inventions is, as explained at length on pp. 168f., not always, nor even usually, effected by competition between societies or cultures and the elimination of one or more competitors as independent entities. Diffusion generally means the adoption by one independent society of innovations initiated by another. But that again is a cumulative process. The adoption of ploughs or of wheeled vehicles in temperate Europe did not mean the elimination of the older hoes or sleds, which in fact continued to fulfil useful, if now more subordinate, functions. It left the rest of the adopting cultures intact save in so far as modifications were needed to accommodate the new techniques of cultivation and transport.

So the result of this rather tedious examination of archæological data is not so negative as at first appeared likely. The concept of cultural evolution as a rational and intelligible process has been vindicated. While the causes of inventions—the circumstances that provoke innovations in tools, in beliefs, in institutions, or in fashions—and of their social acceptance still require elucidation, there is no need to assume supernatural interpositions. Moreover the concept has been clarified by the elimination of false analogies with the processes of organic evolution.

APPENDIX
AND
INDEX

APPENDIX
(See pp. 6-7)

It may be thought that I am not playing fair if I take Mycenæan Greece[1] as my choice example of an advanced barbarian society; for I shall frankly appeal to the Homeric poems to supplement the archæological data. But on the whole this literary testimony will be used only to confirm purely archæological deductions. And the picture thus authenticated is valuable for the interpretation of other cultures that resemble the Mycenæan but are remoter from the literary record.

The standard unit of settlement might be thought to be the fortified acropolis, of which Mycenæ itself is the most famous example. But in reality such acropoles were little more than castles. At Mycenæ, the richest of all, the Cyclopean walls enclosed less than twelve acres, at Tiryns half as much. A large proportion of the fortified area was in every case occupied by a palace with the connected magazines and workshops. The cemeteries imply a much larger population than could conveniently shelter within such a cramped space. They consist of rock-cut collective tombs used by a single family for successive interments for a century or two. Round Mycenæ[2] only some ninety family tombs have been described, but there must be many more. Fifty-five have already been excavated round the much less important citadel of Prosymna,[3] a few miles away. None here are on the acropolis slope; the graves form groups on three adjacent ridges scattered over an area

---

[1] Consult in general, Tsountas and Manatt, *The Mycenæan Age*; Nilsson, *Homer and Mycene* (1933); Myres, *Who Were the Greeks?* (1938).

[2] Wace in *Archæologia* LXXXII (1932).

[3] Blegen, *Prosymna* (Cambridge; 1937), p. 229.

about a kilometre long. The cemeteries at Mycenæ and other sites form equally dispersed groups. In general, each group of tombs is supposed to correspond to a village or cluster of farms outside the city walls but economically and politically dependent upon the citadel. The bulk of the "urban" population must have actually lived in such villages, but there were in addition independent nuclei of habitations, larger or smaller but always more exclusively rural in character. The settlement at Malthi,[1] in Messenia, covered 15,000 m. square and was walled.

The basis of the Mycenæan economy was of course stock-breeding, the cultivation of cereals, and orchard husbandry, particularly the cultivation of olives and vines. Fishing was naturally practised on the coasts and islands, but hunting was mainly a sport for the ruling class. Judged by their products the town populations must have included in addition to primary producers a variety of full-time specialists. Such craftsmen would include not only bronze-smiths and potters using the wheel but also jewellers, engravers, and perhaps tile-makers, as well as other workers, such as wainwrights.[2] Smiths, potters, and some others were presumably permanently resident in every urban centre, but from the Epics we know that experts, like armourers, often travelled about to work for various patrons.

Transport by sea was effected by ships[3] that might attain a length of nearly 100 feet and which were propelled by oars and sails; on land by wheeled vehicles, drawn by horses or oxen, for the passage of which some torrents at least were bridged. (The *Odyssey* suggests no difficulty in driving from Navarino on the west coast across two transverse ranges to Sparta in Laconia!)

[1] Valmin, *The Swedish Messenia Expedition* (Lund; 1938).
[2] Glotz, *Ancient Greece at Work*, p. 44.
[3] Marinatos, in *Bulletin de Correspondence Hellénique*, LVII (1933), pp. 17 ff.

Thanks presumably to these facilities, trade brought to the Mycenæan centres amber from northern Europe, gold, silver, tin, and copper probably from our continent, and manufactures from Egypt, Phœnicia, and Asia Minor. In return Mycenæan pottery has been found in southern Italy, Sicily, and Macedonia, all along the coasts of Asia, and well up the Nile in Egypt. Fayence beads, quite possibly of Mycenæan manufacture and almost certainly transmitted through Mycenæan middlemen, reached the Middle Danube basin, Spain, Brittany, and above all England. These surviving trade-goods represent only a fraction of the total. Exports from Greece probably included wine, olive oil, dyestuffs, and textiles; food-stuffs as well as spices and perfumes may have been imported.

Exchange was expedited by the social recognition of the ox as a standard of value.[1] This is well attested by the Homeric poems, but might have been inferred without that testimony from the fact that ingots of copper of standard weight were cast in the form of an outstretched ox-hide. Specified weights of copper or gold were conventionally equated with the ox unit and its fractions and multiples. No coined money was available, so that the quantities of metal had to be weighed out, and a merchant must carry a balance or steelyard with him (actual specimens survive, though the best known are symbolic scales for the mythical " weighing of souls " in the after life). Small transactions must have been conducted on a basis of barter, and grave-goods and hoards show as clearly as the Epics that wealth was accumulated in the forms of cauldrons, tripods, jewels, and the like.

But piracy has never been clearly contrasted with trade in the Mediterranean world, and, judging by the *Odyssey,* booty from raids may have enriched the Mycenæan Greeks. But internecine warfare between the several local " States "

[1] Seltman, *Greek Coins* (1933), pp. 5-10.

can hardly be regarded as economically productive. Yet, judging by the cyclopean fortifications of the citadels, the prominence of weapons in tombs, and the popularity of battle-scenes in art it may well have been endemic. In spears, tipped and shod with bronze, and long rapiers of addition to slings and bows and arrows we meet plenty of the same metal, as well as great body-shields of bull's hide and helmets of hammered bronze or of leather cased in boar tusks. This metal armament must have been very costly, in view of the relative rarity of copper and tin. But the most decisive arm, judging as much by its prominence in art as by the Homeric descriptions, was the horse-drawn chariot. Now, the fabrication of a light but strong war chariot with the tools available demanded the time and skill of expert craftsmen; the steeds required long training, especially in view of the choking harness used in the Bronze Age. *A priori* one would expect that the possession of horses and chariots was confined to a few who absorbed the social surplus and enjoyed at least the prerogatives of the armoured knight in medieval Europe.

Archæology confirms these expectations. The citadels round which population was grouped were, as we have said, little more than castles largely occupied by palatial apartments. The cemeteries related to each citadel comprise, in addition to the rock-cut family tombs already described, a few " tholoi "—beehive tombs built of fine masonry either in an excavation in a hillside, or on the hilltop and covered with a large round barrow. In contrast to the rock-cut tombs with their numerous interments, each tholos seems normally designed for a single interment, but this, when found intact,[1] was accompanied by a wealth of gear far surpassing in quality as well as quantity anything that accumulated in the tomb of the most prosper-

[1] E.g., at Dendra, Persson. *The Royal Tombs at Dendra near Midea* (Lund; 1931).

ous family. The contrast of palace and tholos with house and rock-cut tomb thus concretely symbolizes the division of Mycenæan society into two classes—ruler and ruled, chieftain and follower, king and subject. The ruler monopolizes the social surplus produced in his own territory and is thus enabled to maintain the armament which not only consolidates his own position but is really essential for the defence of his people against neighbours and foreigners.

This arrangement corresponds exactly to Homeric society dominated by "divine kings" and where battles resolve themselves into single combats between the well-armed chariot-riding princes. At the same time Homer describes Greece as divided up into a vast number of distinct States, all indeed under the hegemony of Agamemnon, king of Mycenæ, and perhaps bound to support him in war, but yet not strictly tributary. Agamemnon is styled "king of men," but not "king of kings," like a Babylonian, Hittite, or Assyrian monarch. So archæologically the fortified centres of population imply a regime where no central power can maintain effective public order over the whole country—or for that matter over even the whole Argive plain. On the other hand, Mycenæ is plainly the richest city. Its rulers are buried in the finest tholos tombs. These, however, are of the same kind as, and only slightly larger and more ornate than, all the many tholoi found in other parts of Greece and as close to Mycenæ as the Argive Heræum and Dendra. Homer's description is needed only to confirm the archæologists' reconstruction of Mycenæan polity.

Even on kinship organization certain deductions are permissible. The rock-cut tomb, containing several corpses buried consecutively but in at least one case all showing a recognizable "family likeness," presupposes the economic independence of the natural family. These tombs form, as we have seen, small cemeteries around each citadel, and in each cemetery the tombs are grouped in smaller clusters. Tsountas[1] suggests that each of the latter may belong to a clan and, rather less convincingly, that each cemetery corresponds to a larger group—a tribe. This is a speculation, but one other detail is established. The Swedish excavators found that in a tholos tomb at Dendra[2] king and queen had been buried simultaneously, each accompanied with equally rich gear. That this points to monogamy for the ruling house is confirmed by Homer. That it indicates *sati* is not so confirmed, but is just as likely as in the earlier example cited. Finally it may be remarked that nothing like a temple has yet been discovered in Mycenæan Greece, and there is no evidence at all for a professional priesthood.

The treasures from the Shaft Graves at Mycenæ and from several tholos tombs show that a Mycenæan or Late Helladic chief could accumulate quite substantial wealth from the dues paid by his followers, gifts from other princes, and booty. At the same time weights and measures had been standardized. Under such conditions writing had been invented in Mesopotamia. Even in Minoan Crete a script and numeral notation had been devised and used in accountancy several centuries before the Mycenæan Age of Mainland Greece began. The Mycenæans borrowed many techniques and devices from the Minoans; fresco-painters, armourers, gem-cutters, and other craftsmen trained in Crete worked in the Mycenæan citadels. But as far as we can judge the art of writing was not generally adopted. Only a few jars with short labels in Minoan letters, a few brief graffiti, and one regular library of account tablets has survived on the mainland; the tablets, discovered at Nestor's capital in 1938, belong to the very last phase of Mycenæan culture. A few literate merchants and craftsmen operated on the Mainland, and

[1] Note 1, p. 46. [2] Note 1, p. 50.

one chief employed a clerk as book-keeper just before the end of the culture. But the Mycenæans seem to have got along without using writing regularly even for economic purposes; there are no indications that historical traditions, scientific observations, or even magic spells were ever written down. So, too, the Homeric poems mention writing but once, and that ambiguously in the phrase "baleful signs."

Thus the Mycenæan culture falls short of the standard we have laid down for civilization. After all, the little citadels with a cluster of hamlets outside their walls belong to a different order of magnitude from the Bronze Age cities of Mesopotamia or India with a walled area of over 100 acres. For all their specialized craftsmen and merchants they are not cities.[1] The accumulation of wealth and population has not reached the critical point. So the utility of our diagnostic criterion—writing—is confirmed and the implication of civilization enriched by this example.

[1] There are some grounds for suspecting that modern towns—e.g. of Argos and Thebes—occupy the sites of Mycenæan towns larger and more "urban" than Mycenæ or Tiryns but yet small in comparison with Ur or Assur.

INDEX

Abydos, 118, 143

Accounting, 133, 149, 156, 184

Agamemnon, 183

Ages, the Three, 28, 30

Al' Ubaid (Mesopotamia), 68, 147

Amber, 63, 94, 105, 111, 122, 131, 181

Amratian Period, 68, 71, 135

Animal husbandry, 89, 158. *See also* Cattle-breeding, Pig-breeding, Sheep-breeding

Anyang, 118

Archaeolithic Age, 75

Area of settlements, villages, cities, etc., 90, 95-6, 98, 123, 139, 151, 185

Aristocracy, 62-3, 80, 115, 127

Art, 78, 80, 134, 164-5

Asses, 138, 149

Bachofen, J., 16

Badarian Period, 135-6, 137, 158

Balance (or steelyard), 181. *See also* Weights

Barbarism, 18, 36, 64

Barrows, *See under* Burial

Beaker-folk, 50, 64, 91, 101, 102, 115, 117

Beds, 54. *See also* Furniture

Blood feuds, 72

Boats, *See* Ships

Boomerangs, 138

Bouffon, 13

Bows and arrows (weapons), 53, 72, 77, 85, 138, 182

Boyne, 61

Broholm, J. C., 63

Bronze, 106

Bucher, K., 16

Burial, 53, 64, 80, 105

barrows, 93, 101, 105, 106, 128, 161

cemeteries, 83, 92, 93, 95-6, 98, 125

chariot graves, 99, 100, 103

collective, 59, 60, 69, 101, 114, 174

double graves, 68, 84, 90, 92, 102, 114, 140, 154

erect, 84

family, 124, 132, 179, 182

megalithic, 104, 116, 161

of chiefs, 85, 115, 118

of rich and poor contrasted, 85

of slaves, 85

royal tombs, 58, 68, 93, 98, 102, 106, 118, 125, 140-1, 161

sati, 53, 68, 84, 85, 100, 162, 171

tholoi, 126, 182

urn-fields, 96

Caesar, Julius, 100

Calendars, 36

Camulodunum (Colchester), 104

Canals, 136, 148

Cannibalism, 15, 76, 80, 82, 96, 102, 162

Capital, 33, 93, 127, 155, 160-1

Castles, 98, 116, 124, 179

Cattle as standard of value, 71

Cattle-breeding, 54, 88, 99, 104, 108, 141, 148. *See also* Animal husbandry

Cattle-byres, 115

Cattle-kraals, 103

Cavalry, 118, 123. *See also* Horse, Warfare

Celts, 68, 160

Cemeteries. *See under* Burial